I0438124

One Year of Insanity

A Woman's Tale of Divorce

Brianna Sannella-Willis

authorHOUSE®

AuthorHouse™
1663 Liberty Drive, Suite 200
Bloomington, IN 47403
www.authorhouse.com
Phone: 1-800-839-8640

© 2009 Brianna Sannella-Willis. All rights reserved.

No part of this book may be reproduced, stored in a retrieval system, or transmitted by any means without the written permission of the author.

First published by AuthorHouse 3/24/2009

ISBN: 978-1-4389-4639-9 (e)
ISBN: 978-1-4389-4637-5 (sc)
ISBN: 978-1-4389-4638-2 (hc)

Library of Congress Control Number: 2009902863

Printed in the United States of America
Bloomington, Indiana

This book is printed on acid-free paper.

Thank you page

For my precious, little Amelie Isabella. My hope rests in your grace, beauty, resilience, and laughter. I pray your heart will always sing, "What a wonderful world". Smiles and silly tears my love.

For my mom, my hope, my peace, my strength.

Contents

Preface

"As human beings, our greatness lies not so much in being able to remake the world ~ that is the myth of the atomic age ~ as in being able to remake ourselves."
~Mohandas Gandhi

*D*are I even question who I am or the fate of my meager little existence for that matter? Why, that would take the unraveling of an entire universe to answer such an abstract, ridiculous question. Even Socrates could not avoid the inevitable death penalty when he attempted to find an absolute truth surrounding these demoralizing questions. Yet, I live in a democratic society, so I must attempt to answer this question while I have the chance.

Those brilliant minds who believed the world of Oceania was the epitome of anarchy must think again. While Orwell's dissertation on chaos, manipulation, and control is revered as a masterpiece, I must argue that my character, the dejected woman who stands before you, would have fashioned a much more perfect leading character.

While this reality may be an absolute truth to me (Even though I do not believe in such a concept), I must be sensitive to those Orwellian minds who believe him to be a prophet. Dare I even speak such blasphemy? While I have never been physically tortured via rats or inhibited by the all powerful Big Brother, I must say at this time in my life-dejected and filled with self-pity-I have committed the most vial sin of all. For at this very moment in time, I have likened myself to Winston-the downtrodden conspirator who caved under pressure and became another number in a world of pathetic, passionless, uneducated heathens, forced to live under the constant scrutiny of a Stanlinesque regime.

I would like to believe that as the main character in my own story, fiction or not, that I have some control over the resolution. Sadly, I have realized that the not-so-compassionate power, Fate, has driven me to the edge of near insanity. The reason behind this dejected reality lies in the fact that I had no control over my own free will (or, I am not ready at this time to accept responsibility). How could one possibly assert his or her own free will when one's reality does not even exist?

As Winston was betrayed by the conniving O'Brien, and Julia for that matter, I too was led to Room 101 by forces unbeknownst to me. That room, which is the place where there is no breathing, became my reality when I realized the only raw truth that existed in my life was a lie. Then, the consciousness of the un-truth led to the same sense of nothingness that tortured Winston after he submitted to a world he despised.

While critics of the acclaimed *1984* will most likely lead a revolt against my comparing little ole' me to such a brilliant fictional protagonist, there is no doubt that in my own insane mind, that which I feared most, my inability to control my own course in life, would haunt me for more hours that I had hoped.

A Sabbatical of the Mind

*"Life is to be lived, not controlled, and humanity is won
by continuing to play in face of certain defeat."*
~Ralph Ellison

*J*t is such an eerie sensation when you wake up one day and realize that the past twelve years have been a farce; a complete figment of one's imagination. Thank god numbness is an emotion, or lack thereof, that accompanies the type of grief that pulls us so far down that even our eyelids cannot seem to fight the ever-powerful center of gravity. Sadly, most will tell us that feeling naturally sedated, which at times seems to be the best frame of mind in which one may exist, is only good for us in increments and for only about twenty percent of the time. So what the hell are we supposed to do with the other eighty percent?

I would love to tell you that I have it all figured out; that 22 percent of the time, we will feel jovial, tempted to run through the most beautiful, lush fields of green at any given moment, feeling a freedom that, even though may be a vague memory, did exist once.

Thirty-seven percent of the time, we will be enticed by our sub-conscious (who, as of late, we always get to blame for our poor, irrational decisions) to run to the nearest liquor store and seize the cheapest bottle of merlot, since it is has become the saving grace for so many of the of divorcees out there who have succumbed to such a ridiculous budget as I have of late. While we are there, as much as we would like to shed the 20 pounds as a result of the divorce diet, that half pint of chocolate ice cream with peanut butter swirled throughout it is taunting us from four isles across the store. Because we have turned into innocent victims constrained by vulnerable states of mind, we have become the bait and are therefore coerced into wasting our precious latte money and buying the high caloric, cellulite-manufacturing anti-depressant. We will then come back home and indulge until there is nothing left but to pass out on the bathroom floor (sounds absolutely riveting. Wait, it only gets better).

Then, of course there is the other 21 percent. This, I have been taught by all of my self-help gurus, is the one that we shall embrace the most-being completely, utterly depressed and allowing ourselves to be absolutely pitiable. "For it is in this absolute suffering, which has been likened to death, that we will grow."

As my three-year-old would say, "WHATEVER."

Is this really going to be my reality for however long it takes me to be even somewhat sensible? I still remember when one of those self-help psychoanalysts told me it would take me double the time I spent with someone to get entirely over them.

My comment to her was, "Are you completely insane? I mean, I know you went to college for years, which everyone knows makes us all brilliant scholars who are experts in their field of study, but this is perfectly ludicrous."

What was really going on in this thwarted mind of mine was, if this is the case, then I am completely obsolete and I may as well hike to the top of Half Dome and take up skydiving without any equipment. Apparently, for some this is completely normal. Why not join them?

After all, I will be fifty-years-old by the time I am over him. By then, my once-elated breasts will sag even farther than my belly button, my peach fuzz that has decided to blossom on my cheeks during this time of pandemonium will compare me to a sasquatch. And those goading underarms of mine? Well, they will incite me to the point of complete turmoil. If I had a hard time dating in my early twenties, I cannot wait until I am finally over him. I have so much to look forward to over the next twenty-four years. Hooray!"

No! This cannot possibly be my reality for the next 24 years. It just is not humane. Actually, it is not even justifiable for anything that is not human. So, how do I get through this heartrending point in my life where I have become the protagonist in the most nauseating and obnoxious horror-meets-cheesy romance fiction novel of all time?

The answer is, "I am not going to."

You and your resilient, brilliant mind are of course asking me, "Then what is the point?"

Great question. You see the truth is, I am not going to *get* through it.

> ත I am going to abhorrently bawl my way through it.
> ත Occasionally, I will viciously laugh my way through it (Yes, there must always be laughter).
> ත I may take on another life form, run down to the nearest Rawhide Saloon and inebriate my way through it.

- I may psychotically hunt-down-those-people-who-are-the-reason-for-my-hurt-and-reduce-their-lives-to rubble-my way through it.
- At times, I will most likely be completely insane and irrationally temper-tantrum my way through it. There will only be a few of these instances because I *always* have it together in real life.
- I will probably consume a million calories in one day and gobble my way through it. Did I really just liken myself to a turkey?
- And yes, I may even one-night-stand my way back to sanity. Ok, so you may already sense that I am all talk. Hold on to that truth, as that may be the only thing I in all honestly know about myself at the prudent age of twenty-seven.

I did just say that, out loud, didn't I?

So you see dear reader, nobody merely gets through such an uncouth turning point in their life. When one is forced to succumb to the crude, indecent trenches of life without being able to, at any moment, crawl out of it and catch even a glimpse of what used be a typical day in the life of a somewhat sane person, they don't just deal.

I (now remember, I am still trying to find my way back to sanity and may not be an expert on this topic) do not feel it wise to pretend that the only way to rise out of the one, two, three years, or even a lifetime of insanity is to adhere to a belief that they must seem like they have it all together. You will find in my memoir of this past one-full-year of complete, unquestionable lunacy, that there was no perfect, absolute step-by-step system in place in order to emerge into the whole, rational woman I have become.

Which brings me to another topic-do not believe everything a person writes. For it would be foolish to believe that any person on this silly planet has it *all* together. It is also absurd to assume that every person who is faced with a demoralizing divorce will handle their grief in the same way.

You may disagree, and I am perfectly ok with that. That thick skin that Dean continually discussed with me, has finally decided to develop.

Some of you more astute readers may hold tight to the conviction that there are five, six, or even 12 steps from which every person must graduate with honors in order to become an upright, first-class citizen with good judgment. I urge you though, to think of me as your devil's advocate and take part in a forum on the raw truth about divorce. There *truly* is no real method to sanity after divorce. It is also a bona fide *truth* that it is one of those times in our lives where there is a fierce battle between the rational and irrational. This is the most intense, heated war where one side of the mind is the brave, lion-hearted Odysseus and the other the stoic, thick-headed Poseidon, each unyielding to any idea that they may be wrong in their quest for justice.

For those of you who are seeking advice from this non-self-help expert on love and the sudden rapture of it, you will most likely not find it here. What you will discover, which hopefully will be of some condolence to you, is that you really are not the only life form on the planet who has strangely started conversing with some bizarre voice that seems to only be heard by you.

For the rest of you who have it much more together, all I can say is, "Good for you. Go climb to the highest mountain you can find and yell out to the world that you are not crazy and are therefore indebted to the gods for helping you maintain the ultimate form of sanity." Yet, I assure you, even if you are in a serene place right now, there may be a point in your life where you are entangled in a gross reality where there is nothing else to do but to incessantly talk to something that cannot be seen. Whether you like it or not, there is a huge chance that you too will one day be lured into a complete madness. When you do, I, and my intrusive, omniscient friend (yes, he does become my friend), will be here ready to share in the ill-omened chapter of your life.

Until then, please take heart and be open to the fact that what you are about to read stems from a modest chapter in *my* life that not even the awe-inspiring, powerful forces of nature could terminate.

The First Night

A meeting of the sane and insane; or
rather the rational and irrational

*"Insanity: doing the same thing over and over
again and expecting different results."*
~Albert Einstein

"**Y**ou must stop crying."

"Are you serious?"

"You are really starting to look haggard. I highly suggest you stop crying."

"I told you, I can't. And, for the record, my puffy eyes look fabulous with this hue of pink."

"Stop crying."

"I cannot. And, if I could, I'm not quite sure it would do anything for me. Plus, I did hear once that tears, which are the perfect combination of salt and water, do wonders for the complexion, which I have been putting off as of late because of my highly-toxic stress levels."

"Get off of the floor, stand up, put your shoulder's back, and lift your chin. I have noticed that you have been sitting there, night after night, for at least a couple of weeks. It is time for me to intervene and take action."

"My head won't lift, my eyes won't open, and my lungs are not taking in any air. So please, tell me when I am supposed to get up off of this floor. Am I just magically going to grow gigantic wings, lift off and go hang out with the man on the moon? Maybe he can read me his eloquently-written dissertation on the meaning of life. Or better yet, maybe I can ask Daedalus to build me some paranormal wings. That sure did a lot of good for Icarus, didn't it?"

"Shake it off. You are resilient and really need to get it together. Get on with life."

"What if I don't want to? What if all I want to do is sit here, in this desolate, austere corner of the earth and cry? What if I want to be belligerent, pathetic, dreadful? If I sit here long enough, maybe I won't be anymore. Maybe if I stare at that image-filled wall, I will become a part of it; just an on-looker into this cruel, meaningless interim of life. I won't take up any more breathing space and maybe for once I will feel liberated, not suffocated."

"Yes, but what about her? She depends on you and her love is unconditional. She needs you."

"And?"

"What?"

"How do I begin to show her what my love is? Am I even capable of it? Really. Am I? How could I possibly be when my heart has placed a 'vacancy' sign over it in bold, neon lights?"

"Your heart? That small thing is not even yours. What makes you think you have any control over it anyway? You have become so lax. Your perceptions, judgments, which used to be somewhat clear, are now so flaccid. Are you there?"

"Quasi-here, I think."

"Stand up. Get into bed, drink that glass of red wine (that you have neglected and has therefore been visiting with Mrs. Karenina over there) and then ask Mr. Tolstoy how they endured life's trepidations. I am sure he has some advice on the topic of love, or its paradoxical non-existence that seems to be the theme that you have created at this moment."

"Why the hell should I have to deal with these painful pangs of consciousness? Every moment, every second I sit here, my thoughts trigger words like 'regret', 'shame', 'guilt'. They keep playing over and over in my mind, like a horrible 1980s rendition of long lost love and pitiful broken hearts. The record keeps going, while I sit and the words twist, slant, slide, and jump up and down, as if they are taunting me. If I could only have a forceful conversation with them? Then I remember, wait, I am not capable of assertiveness. That "Assertiveness Training" with the $75-dollars-and-hour-therapist did not work. In fact, I think I have become more of a weakling. Well, this is just great. I feel like my fit is going to get worse."

"Wow, you really are going to lose your mind aren't you? Do I need to call in the armed forces?"

"Actually, the mafia might be able to help. Wait, I definitely should not go there. This is about me, not him."

"You are right."

"No, I am not. He should be off'd. This is all about him."

"Wait a second. I will have to disagree."

"Go ahead. But your disagreeing is going to cause you much heartache-and your life's savings. It is so hard to admit, 'I am wrong, you are right, and I am sorry,' which is something you are definitely going to have to say. I am quite positive you are not going to want to spend as much money as I did to learn how to admit to this invention of false humility."

"You have become quite the cynic as of late, haven't you?"

"Not really "quit the cynic" but rather, an "absolute cynic". Do you have a problem with this?"

"No, I am just confused. Everyone I seem to come into contact with has this idea that you, mam, are quite the opposite."

"First of all, I would appreciate it if you did not call me 'mam'. For I am far too young to be called such and prefer to be called 'miss.' And, for the record, I feel completely comfortable being a cynic. How could I not be? Someone who has had their heart ripped, yes literally ripped, from their body most likely cannot see the so-called joyous adventures that life so mysteriously brings to us at any given moment."

"Well, I do apologize, if that is of any condolence to you, miss?"

"Good, we may continue our conversation.

'As I was saying, I did seem to have an extremely utopian view of life once. I remember it clearly. Sadly, I had to jump out of a small, six-passenger airplane to find it, but it did exist. As I jumped into a very large space called air, I was perfectly at peace. Alone, yes. But, peace existed for me. It was beautiful. In fact, I am not sure you are worthy of my truly explaining it to you. Yet, you are starting to grow on me, so I will.

'As I looked down and saw this green and blue canvas, that was quite breathtaking and must have been created by some brilliant artist, I saw me. I was this small speck; a trivial ingredient in the Artist's picturesque landscape. I realized that while every other organ in my body was probably completely out of whack, my heart was perfectly in tact. I was truly at peace. Me, the air, which could not do much talking, and the brilliant Artist. That was it. I did not need anyone, or anything else, to fill any dark void, or luminous one at that, in my life. Then, upon landing, which thank goodness was a graceful one, unrelenting reality sustained. I heard voices-many of them.

'Now, I have always held to this belief that people are innately good. Even in my desperate moment of hopelessness, I truly do hold to this conviction. Well, partially. Ok, I know I am sounding fickle, but write all of this down. This is the cause of many of my problems. Maybe that therapist was ingenious. We will get to that discussion later.

'As I was saying, while my only true moment of peace existed by myself, this should give me some condolence to my newfound life. Wow, that was quite the contradiction. It is not like I 'found' this life. *He* found it for me, among other things.

'All right, where is the mafia? May we call in the militia as well please? Great, here go those thoughts again. Will they every stop?"

"It is not about *him*, remember."

"Fine. As I was saying, again, I have always found an immense sense of peace being alone. So, why is it so different now? I can say it is because *he* is not. Yet, that is an extremely juvenile statement. God forbid *I*, the one who has always had it all together, be immature.

'So, I must put these inane thoughts back into my, as Freud, who apparently was some brilliant guy who had it all together (if one such exists), would call it, below-level-of-consciousness state, and forget that they exist. Of course, this may lead to my demise, but it is what feels comfortable right now. Don't you agree?"

"I am not sure what I agree with anymore."

"I concur."

"What?"

"Never mind. I am finished with this conversation right now. Thank you for assisting in alleviated this pain that runs through every inch of my 'lifeless', yet sometimes 'full-of-too-much-life' body of mine. Can't I just become numb, like *him*. Wouldn't that be nice."

"No."

"Why not?"

"Because you are not *him*, and *he* is not you. Don't you realize that? Are you ever going to realize that? People are who they are and there is no changing that."

"Why do you have to be so right, and eloquent about everything?"

"Good night."

"Sweet dreams."

"Godspeed. You are definitely going to need it. Hopefully, we can fast forward to a place where you are not so pathetic."

"Thanks a billion. I will see you again. Three o'clock. A.M. Same corner of this depressing, lonely, bleak room. Me and you."

11

The Second Night

Am I still here?

"Each one has to find his peace from within. And peace to be real must be unaffected by outside circumstances."
~Mohandas Gandhi

"**I**s that you again?"

"Yes, it is. You, miss, do not look so great. How long have you been lying on that cool, sinister floor?"

"Why do you continue to taunt me? I have only been on the ground for a few hours, which is much better than days, I suppose. I am starting to get somewhere.

'I am not quite sure how I got here. The past few weeks seem to be a complete blur. All I do is work, run, try my best to be a mom, clean, and cry. I am one big, jumbled pathetic mess. Some say that the running, out of all of the former verbs, is a sign of strength. I say it is metaphorical for the summation of my life. I run. I run far, far away from what hurts me and from what is good for me. Please tell me how this so-called asset of mine is going to help me? Also, please enlighten me as to how, at this moment, while everyone is soundly sleeping, I am going to even pretend that I can ascend any farther than the foot of my bed (who, by the way, has also abandoned me in the midst of all of this chaos) and pretend to be a woman of strength and courage?

'My mother always tells me this is the true, denotative meaning of my name. She would be drawn into a deep state of sadness to see that her 'perfect' child has sunken into a place where strength seems to mean *fragile* and the meaning of courage has taken up a new adjective; *weakling*. My God, I hope she never hears this conversation we are having. She may suddenly be thrust into this deplorable state of reality, which I refuse to believe I created myself."

"Wait a second, you keep reverberating the notion that it is someone else's fault that you are here. I am emphatically trying to understand this assertion that it someone else's burden to bear that you have become a withdrawn, saddled, runoholic with droopy eyes and an unforgivable complexion. Is it truly the fault of another human being that you have become afflicted by the kind of gloominess that could send the entire country into an emotional recession?"

"Why, yes it is. I did not make the conscious, appalling decision to go out and live the good life with Suzie so-and-so and the latest Zane's rendition of what the people of Tuolumne County might call a hottie-tottie. You truly do have the sagacity to even question this?"

"Since you are deciding to be so haughty on this early morning, I will give it right back to you. As a matter of fact, I am questioning why you have committed the most appalling crime of all-that five-letter-word, *blame*? As your rational friend (yes, someday you will come to the raison de'être that I am, in fact, your faithful friend who, while you will abandon at times, is always present in your life) I must be completely candid with you. This dreadful position that you find yourself in at this moment cannot be blamed on anyone else. The liability is not found in any particular person."

"Are you absolutely mad? What species, other than the pigheaded ones, leave their families and frolic off to greener, or blonder pastures, to be able to experience true bliss? For god's sake, even penguins are willing to tread through ice and life-threatening storms for the women they cherish. Am I asking too much from a human being? "

"The person of whom you are so irrationally gauging must not be judged or charged with such offenses until you are ready to do so. For, they are the ones who are not quite sure who they are yet. The ones who, every night, after leaving their safe haven that seems to bring them joy and fulfillment, go home and find that the place where their heart once existed has become paradoxically barren. The ones who find a bleak interim between what *is* real and what they want to believe is real. Am I making any sense to you?"

"I am so tired of hearing this from those self-proclaimed, have-it-all-together, know-all analysts. No offense Mr. Tesh, but I have found there is something worse than going to the dentist; going to see Mr. Ronneberg (who is, in fact, a very gentle tooth tradesman) and sitting through an entire filling listening to your expertise on what to eat, how to love, when to be bold, and where to sit when at an exquisite dinner date setting. I must ask, do you heed to all of this 'brilliant' advice that the dear people of America so patiently wait for on the hour, every hour?

'Your answer is 'no'. Why I am not surprised is just that, not surprising.'

"Wow that was quite the rant, Miss Angry at the Wrong Person. What did Tesh do to you to make you so bitter and borderline psychotic at the same time? Sounds like someone is jealous that Mr. T got airtime while you, my almost-friend, became a lowly wannabe who ended up in the boondocks selling yourself to those real estate agents you love so much."

"Sorry, I am being a bit irrational I guess. He does have a nice sounding voice and his intentions are probably completely true. Yet I can't help but feel guilty whenever he, or any other smarty pants, like Dr. Phil and his perfect wife, opens their mouth. What makes them so stable and the rest of us to hysterically insane? How do I achieve such peace and tranquility? If I did attain it, would I even like it? So many inquiries, so little brain room in which to even attempt to answer these life-altering questions."

"I know they all sound a little arrogant, but there is some method to their madness, I suppose."

"Yep. To make all of us question who we are, constantly, to get a bigger bang for their buck."

"No, you crazy cynic. To try to give the ones who are perched on the edge of life's hemisphere, waiting to jump into the realm of non-existence just to escape having to figure out the answers themselves, an easier way out of the dark hole of depression."

"What happened to the good-old question, 'To be, or not to be.' Even Hamlet, who had complete grounds for searching for a way out of this stir-crazy place, stopped to question his existence and then found a way to combat his own problems without the help of 20 books balancing on his nightstand, each with 48 bunny ears highlighting where to turn if you are contemplating moving onto stage three of the grief process too soon without first completely finishing stage two (God forbid you ever go out of sequence)."

"You do have a point."

"Of course I do, I am a brilliant scholar."

"Who has obviously suffered amnesia and forgotten she has a degree in journalism, not physics."

"Are you saying, my never-going-to-be-my friend-now-acquaintance, that I have no business touching on life's most meaningful topic of existence just because I have a meager little degree in writing (which apparently has become the equivalent of a 1st grade diploma)."

"At least they can write complete, non-fragmented sentences that are not so obscure and filled with such angry tones."

"Point taken. Now that I am feeling even worse about myself than I was this morning when I found the $800-dollar phone bill with the 2400 text messages and 4 0'clock in the morning phone calls to Mary, Jane, and Cindy, I will just take my last sip of red-red wine and drift off to dream of what life would have been like if I had just stayed in Paris."

"What?"

"I am sure at the rate we are going, that we will have plenty of time to discuss that turning point in my life. *Le Mort de Destin* is the title I have given it. You may sleep on that.

'Bonjour."

"Bonjour, femme ètrange."

"There goes that sarcasm again. I highly recommend you heed to my advice on the touchy topic. You are lucky there are no phones in sight. By the way, I prefer to be called *une belle femme*, thank you very much. It just suits me much better."

The Third Night

I cannot possibly be this crazy

"We do not grow absolutely, chronologically. We grow sometimes in one dimension, and not in another; unevenly. We grow partially. We are relative. We are mature in one realm, childish in another. The past, present, and future mingle and pull us backward, forward, or fix us in the present. We are made up of layers, cells, constellations."
~Anais Nin

"**I**s that you?"

"It sounds like you are starting to warm up to me. Where does this strange, out-of-character, affable tone come from?"

"I really am not sure I'm up for sarcasm right now. I lived with that for far too long, to the point of complete insanity. Actually, to the point of phone-throwing. Yes, I am admitting another ridiculous fault of mine that few know about the mellow, passive miss that sits barren before you. I have never been one to lash out in anger or say painful, unkind words (Once again, I am hoping that expensive assertiveness training will guide me to bolder places). I will tell you though, when the same person, whose name I dare not mention, comes at me with barbed wire (the metaphorical kind) and lashes at my soul, phones will be thrown."

Warning to future betrothed, sarcasm equates a whole other realm of irrationality.

"Any other faults you would like to throw out there?"

"Don't push it. This humility stuff takes much time. I have only known you for about five weeks. Also, are humans even capable of humility?"

"Yet again, another bleak, wild thought has tainted your once-innocent soul."

"Innocent! At birth *maybe.* By the way, I feel that I am perfectly permitted to question life, love, and the pursuit of happiness, as well as anything that comes in my way of that. Worked for all of those smart guys I taught in school, didn't it?"

"Maybe within acceptable limits."

"Which brings up another topic, why are 99 percent of the authors and so-called brilliant thinkers men. I guess there is no hope for me. Great, here I go again."

"Yep."

"What the heck does that mean? Now you, my rational friend, are not starting to make sense. If you wish to hang out with me until 3:30 on this tolerable morning, then I suggest you take up the part of the reasonable one."

"So, what really has dragged you down to the spot on the floor below the cool, refreshing portrait of fluorescent poppies in a wide-open, lush field? Aren't you an English teacher? I may not be some ingenious high school teacher, as they all are, but I did read once one of that Frost's guys poems, and it seemed like flowers, spring, and all of that nature stuff symbolizes new life, joy, and self-reflection. Why aren't you jumping on his bandwagon?"

"If you read, 'Two Roads,' smartass, you might understand. I chose the one often-traveled."

"Ok, explains everything. Back to why I am here. I really need to know why you are here, *again.*"

"My question exactly? Now you know, my new acquaintance (we will get to 'friend' sooner or later, if you are lucky), I am not supposed to be here. If fate had its way and I wasn't so darn stubborn and self-consumed, then maybe I would have taken the latter road. I will tell you where fate had me. Fate had me:

- ❧ In Barbara Walter's seat touching the lives of so many men and women, saving the world one rich, famous, or crazy person at a time (I guess I may have had to interview myself then-would have been a first-absolutely ingenious).

- ❧ A famous writer for *The New York Times*, spanning the globe, treading through war-torn countries trying to find the most current, touching, compassionate story ever written. It would have been such too, if the whole free will thing had not been invented.

- ❧ A reporter for Sacramento's awe-inspiring Channel 3 News. 'This is Brianna Willis, signing off.' I guess I got to use that one later on in life, didn't I?

- ❧ A teacher in Malawi, creating a sense of hope in a grief-stricken world.

- ❧ A master's student studying under the ingenious professors of Berkeley University. I know they only accept six students a year, but come on. You must admit that fate stuff is pretty powerful.

- ◈ A professor of literature at a brilliant university, studying Dostoevsky, Hesse, and Dreiser.
- ◈ A world traveler.
- ◈ A wife, someday. Married to the most loving, selfless, handsome man on the planet (I have not lost hope in the midst of all of this mayhem that one such exists. Where is my Wentworth?).
- ◈ A mom of one. Call me crazy, but I didn't succumb to the pressures of having 2.4 children.

'Anywhere but here in this crazy, everyone-knows-everything-about-you part of the earth.

'Don't you see, it was all planned out in flawless penmanship on crisp, colorful paper.

'And yet, here I am. I have succumbed to the deepest trenches of life. I am an English teacher on sabbatical. No, not the kind of sabbatical where you leave to find serenity and inspiration to come back and become the most enthusiastic, motivating teacher on the planet, stirring up a sense of peace and self-worth in our youth of today.

No, I am talking about the kind where you are running. This is where that whole running metaphor comes back into play. I thought, since I did not have the time to be the best teacher, I would run to the next item on my list-an awe-inspiring, life-changing, empathetic, loan officer.

'You are laughing?"

"I am merely laughing with you my dear friend. I highly recommend you choose different adjectives to describe your newfound profession. For you, miss, have been completely duped into believing you are some humanitarian changing the world one greedy character at a time."

"Of this I am completely aware, smarty pants. But thank you for clueing me in on a newfound reality that is going to cause me to plunge even farther down into the deep trenches of wretchedness."

"Just trying to keep you in check with what is real."

"Job well done. Unless I have unexpectedly come across the perfect anecdote to cure my madness, I will see you tomorrow morning."

The Fourth Night
Madness still abounds

"We must develop and maintain the capacity to forgive. He who is devoid of the power to forgive is devoid of the power to love. There is some good in the worst of us and some evil in the best of us. When we discover this, we are less prone to hate our enemies."
~Martin Luther Kind, Jr.

"*G*ood morning my self-proclaimed senseless friend."

"I am so glad you are here."

"What?"

"Don't push it. The reality is, I really needed you right now, and here you are. I am starting to think that you are my saving grace; someone sent on the most bizarre charity mission and for some reason, you submitted without first checking into what the assignment really entailed.

'You keep surprising me at the very moments where I have dwindled (both literally and figuratively) into a minuscule organism that cannot even face up to the reality at hand."

"Have you been sitting here, under that poppy picture, all week?"

"Actually, the past week was manageable, which must have been the very reason for your absence. Not a whole lot of laughing or smiling. Yet, on a good note, not too much crying or running either. For the first time since I found that wretched phone bill and discovered I was not the only blonde in his life, I was able to find a balance between utter craziness and near sanity.

'Wait, there was one episode in my uneventful life that caused my side to split in more places than one. I suppose, if I wasn't in this situation right now, it would not have been so extremely hilarious. If you knew me well, my almost-friend, and all of my prudish ways, you might also find it quite comical."

"You a prude, I have not sensed that you from you yet."

"Remember what I have said about sarcasm, and the unadulterated aftermath of it?"

"Point could not even be a little better-taken."

"May I proceed?"

"Uh, huh."

"I was sitting on my ever-faithful, compassionate couch the other night and I got dreadfully fed up with running away from reality. So, with all of the excitement I could conjure up on a Friday night, I decided to go downstairs and open that wretched tin box that sits alone (there is a definite reason for his desolation). My god, it is amazing what one week of abandoning my enemy can cause. There was a heap of paperwork that amassed in the 8 x 10 inch crafty reality organizer. You would think after not coming to his aide and relieving him of the belly-filling junk, he would have just thrown it back up and scared off the ever-faithful mailman.

'No, he didn't and to my dismay, none of the local high-schoolers decided to wreak havoc in my neighborhood and take my mailbox for ransom.

'I grabbed what had become my miserable reality-check, and went back to my couch. It was then that I noticed *it*-my tormenting, monthly acquaintance. Her haunting eyes were glaring at me through the window, saying, 'Open me with caution. Another world of lunacy lies behind the safety net of this envelope.'"

"Well, did you open it? Or did you save yourself from the unsympathetic reality that you knew existed in the other realm of your once-cushioned life?"

"I opened it. To my non-surprise, the pages were endless. The numbers, and there were many of them, were callous and seemed to be dancing around, goading at me as if they were thrilled that I actually knew they existed. You would think after three monthly cycles of this, that he would at least prance down to the nearest Cingular and open his own account. My lord, what is he trying to do?"

"I can't believe you are even contemplating being surprised. I know I have never met this other half of your insanity, but I will tell you, there must be a merciless side to this other life form as well."

"We could muster up some other descriptive words for him, but I will not give it the time of day, or morning at that, to ponder on such a lowly mortal."

"Calm down, rash one. Remember, this is not the time in your irrational state of mind to be harboring anger toward someone, or something, that you do not understand. Trust me, there will be plenty of time to act out that frame of mind. This just isn't it."

"I will heed to your advice, I suppose.

'After a few minutes of evaluating the non-sensical, asinine reality that lay before me, I heard a knock on the door.

'There he stood, in all of his ridiculous glory. I swear he thought he was some knight in shining armor come to sweep the poor, sad, lonely woman, who must have forgotten about all of the devious, amoral deeds that took place, off of her feet. Well, I hate to admit another one of my defects, but I gave in to those agonizingly-manipulative brown eyes of his. Thank god I didn't give into any other part of his anatomy, for that would have taken away even the smallest amount of my pride I have left at this point in my life."

"Don't tell me, after two months of him being gone, that you let him through your door."

"The fault is not mine. For the door, in all her majestic beauty, knows better than any human being what took place the day she hit him in the behind. She should have had much more strength than to let him in. But, nonetheless, she did. And she would be sorry, or highly entertained that she did so.

'After a few minutes of him lamenting over his newfound life, that apparently he did not bring upon himself, I yet again gave in and offered a warm shower and a place to do his laundry. I know I should have told him to have one of his new Zane's girls do it for him, but remember, I am far too passive for that. Instead, I decided to write a song for him, 'Requiem for a poor, sad, cheating spouse.' I was so utterly sad for this creature who I once vowed to love and cherish and blah, blah, blah forever. Until…

'There they were. Those numbers were haunting me from the eternal, effervescent junk drawer. I tried to shove them away the minute I heard the door knock, but they would follow me wherever I went. I tried to repress my feelings, to forget that they existed. I even attempted, for a split second, to become one of those people I envy so much who are able to just let it all go. And, remember that small dissertation about how people do not change. Well I am quite confident that this part of my personae will never change either. I am dreadfully bad at sweeping debauchery under the rug-especially when it is aimed at me."

"Am I going to have to keep telling you that none of these depravities have ever been directed toward you? When did you get so narcissistic to believe that someone would actually spend incessant hours trying to screw up *your* life? What makes you so important?"

"You know, you don't have to be so mean-spirited."

"Moving along…"

"OK, remember our discussion about the phones. Well, there is another behavior that I do not like to admit to the masses; I am a door slammer. You must admit though, where there is a phone-thrower, there is a door-thrower. I must adhere to this cliché. I suppose. I don't want to be the one responsible for throwing the universe out of whack, so I hold to my conviction that if I am going to be a door slammer, I must do it with wild conviction.

'So, upon being lured by the black numbers on the once pure piece of white paper, I went over to the junk drawer and pulled out the 17 accomplices to the crime. My heart, which used to be in tact, now began pulling in a forward motion. The inertia alone drove me to a whole new realm of existence. I asked myself what the hell I was doing allowing this thing (the only pronoun that comes to mind nowadays) to be graced by the comfort that accompanies such a place as mine.

'With the only thing but a towel in tact, the thing stepped outside the ever-faithful front door to run downstairs and grab some clothes out of his four-wheeled closet. Me, not wanting to be someone that I am not, ran straight to the front door, slammed her, and locked the dead bolt.

'This may seem completely childish…"

"Yes, it does."

"Thank you. As I was saying, because you were not there to tame me, my irrational mind took over and I succumbed to complete immaturity. But, my goodness it felt fabulous. There is a sense of liberation when you know the person who caused your heart to file bankruptcy is standing in the rain, freezing his innards, and outards off (which may have been a good thing). There he stood, sopping wet with nothing but a small towel wrapped around his ice-cold body, begging me to let him in. I was finally in charge and was not going to release any sense of control I had over this impoverished, heartless entity.

'It was then, in my moment of complete bliss, that my worse nightmare came true. I could hear the faint screams of the sirens in the distance. Did he really have the audacity to call the cops on me-poor, innocent, prudish, have-never-even-had-a-speeding-ticket-soon-to-be-divorcee?

'Yep, he did. And they came in full force, ready to extinguish the inhumane person who dare throw an always-innocent correctional officer out of *his* house. I will tell you this was the first time my assertiveness training actually decided to emerge. Sadly, these were not the men to test it on, especially when it is the law that they side with another man in uniform instead of his crazy, fanatical soon-to-be ex-wife. I could tell, it took everything they had not to drag me down to the doghouse that night.

'Needless to say, he got his way-*again*. I did not. But, seeing him shiver in the freezing cold, begging for my mercy, was breathtaking; worth the small section of print devoted to me, the wild, yet oh-so innocuous me, in the Union Democrat."

"Wow, what a highly-treasured fifteen minutes of fame."

"If you think about it, those fifteen minutes of fame, considering I do live in Tuolumne County, probably lasted at least 24 hours, especially when those church-goin'-stay-at-home-moms got a hold of it. Oh, yeah, I'm famous all right."

"I think that third glass of merlot tonight has set you off the top. I think you really need to drown yourself on that pillow over there."

"Sounds absolutely dreamy, no punt intended."

"Good night. After our conversion tonight, I am sure it will be completely necessary to convene tomorrow."

The Fifth Night

Co-dependency is not always such a bad idea, is it?

*"It is to the credit of human nature, that, except where its
selfishness is brought into play, it loves more readily than
it hates. Hatred, by a gradual and quiet process, will even
be transformed to love, unless the change be impeded by a
continually new irritation of the original feeling of hostility."*
~Nathaniel Hawthorne

"*Y*ou promised you would be here tomorrow. Well, it is tomorrow and you are nowhere in sight. This crazy part of my brain is on an uncontrollable rampage again and I really need a sane voice right now. Being that it is two o'clock in the morning, I cannot call anyone. Besides, I'm sure I would run them off if they actually knew what was going on in my head. I cannot stand to lose one more person I love.

'Me and my narcissistic mind are wondering what on earth you have better to do than to sit here with me, in this void room with one diminutive candle lit, exacerbating the dreamy ambiance that once existed? If I sit here and sing, 'Hey there Deliliah' one more time, pretending my Wentworth is going to suddenly parade through my front door and whisk me off of my feet, my heart is going to coagulate and break into a million insignificant pieces.

'I need you, now. You are not allowed to abandon me in a time of blatant absurdity. That must only be left to human beings-the really malicious ones.

'Now, you may be sarcastic, cool, and a bit facetious at times, but you are not heartless. This seems ironic, considering you don't even have a body and are therefore most likely incapable of possessing a heart. Yet, the empty vessel that speaks to me and guides me through most of my inane thoughts must be thanked wholeheartedly, because life form or not, you have been my guide.

'Unless there are storerooms housing hundreds more entities like you, you might want to make haste and come to my aide as soon as I can say, insane."

"Well, that was quite the tirade, my eccentric friend. I told you I would always be here, waiting in full armor to help attack your worst bouts of depression and fanatical behaviors.

'Your position on the floor is much more peculiar than usual and your tone of voice is considerably grave, especially when compared to most other nights. Also, you are much less mocking. Yes, I said it. I know you despise such an idea, but even you too my friend, have the tendency to be a bit sarcastic at times.

'The air of this very room, which I have unintentionally inhabited over the past few months, is daunting as well. Why has everything so quickly changed over the course of just a few hours? I am usually able to leave you for at least a week. While your life is always in slight disorder, it has never been in the frightening state of chaos as it is this morning. Please tell me what lies at the source of all of this mayhem."

"I spoke with her."

"Her?"

"Yes, her, the charlatan who completely deceived me and therefore turned my entire life into the frigid state of confusion it now finds itself."

"This situation is peculiar to me. Let me make sure I have my facts correct. This she, whom you have always refused to discuss, is now the core of all of your problems? Wow, she surely does have much pull over your life now, doesn't she? Well, that is just an absolutely uncanny way of thinking. Actually, it is just quite outrageous."

"Are you calling me weird? I assure you this is no way to try to make a friend."

"If you want to look at it that way, well then yes, you are way out there. I highly recommend you not allow some young temptress to con you into forgetting who you are; do not become duped into believing that someone else can have so much control over your feelings and your utmost raw emotions. It is when you unknowingly or purposely permit someone to invade your mind, conquer it, and seize any reasoning you may have had, that you lose all sense of self and, well, anything really."

"For goodness sake, does the name on my birth certificate read Faust? I certainly do not need his sidekick, Mr. Mephistopheles hanging out with me on a daily basis. For some bizarre reason, Faust asked to be tormented by such a spirit in order to find meaning in his mundane life. All I have asked for is a little bit of rationality looming over me.

'Why I have been deprived of common sense over the past few months is completely beyond me. So forgive me if I am slightly impetuous when it comes to emotions and thinking. I have been highly reckless since I learned about the incessant phone calls at all hours of the day, and night for that matter. Now the abrupt surfacing of a reality that I am not even sure I can confront has converted me into a senseless maniac who cannot manage her nerves, let alone her feelings.

'All I want to do is lay here in this dark room so no one can tell me it is going to be all right. Why is everyone around me lying? Apparently their superegos never had the chance to develop and therefore, they are walking ids ready to strike at any moment. Evidently I have become the perfect wounded target. They now have someone to shoot their impulsive, kill-or-be-killed words toward without thinking twice about it. It is clear that life is not even going to be tolerable. This crazed, so-called miracle has become entirely cruel and futile."

"Wow that was an intense speech. We might want to title it the *dissertation of the most extraordinary kind.* And I don't mean the kind of extraordinary that connotes something even remotely positive.

'I can see that you really need me to just listen right now, correct?"

"Please. I have never felt this degree of pain before. I genuinely do not have a clue as to what to do right now. Before you got here, I was quite the pathetic sight. Now, I am indisputably wretched.

'After stepping through my ever-faithful front door, my legs became completely feeble. I stumbled to my room and tried to permanently place myself in the fetus position; anywhere I would be safe and become, even if for a moment, the epitome of innocence. Upon the realization that I was neither of the two, I fell onto the floor and have taken up shop ever since."

"What time was that?"

"Four in the afternoon."

"What time is it now?"

"Around two o'clock in the morning. I had to beckon you a little earlier than usual. I have never felt so weak and after hours of lying here, I still do not have any answers as to how to pull myself up off of this floor and into bed. Even if I could elevate my lifeless body to the bed, I may have to be heavily sedated in order to fall into a short-term coma and escape this dreaded reality."

"I know you are not so good at opening up to people and becoming absolutely raw, permitting any and all of your emotions, philosophies, feelings to emerge from the foundation of your soul. Yet, I must contend that it is finally time for you to become a real person and admit where your unaffected misery stems from."

"She had been here, there, and everywhere with him."

"What?"

"Could I be bolder in my choice of words? This person, whom I always believed was just a voice on the other end, was actually a true, uninhibited imposter who apparently had nothing else better to do than to come into our lives and weave her web. I keep wishing the story would end like Penelopeia's; the unadulterated woman unweaving her web for truth's sake.

'My reality would not have such a favorable ending."

"You spoke with this so-called Machiavellian today?"

"I did. Aside from my first, bitter tone, to my utmost surprise, she was not as conniving as I thought she would be.

'In my first conversation with her, she was unkind and denied any involvement in the life of my companion that I was supposed to devote my life to for eternity. This time, four months later, she was much more soft-spoken and exhibited a humility that certainly caught me off guard. Her heart, like mine, had been dejected.

'Like this defeated woman who I once portrayed as a man-stealing harlot who shattered my family, I too was humbled to the point of complete conviction. I will not excuse her for making the choice she did, as it is never acceptable to betray someone and wreak havoc in the lives of *innocent* by-standards. Instead, I will make an effort to be compassionate and understand that every person, at different crossroads in their lives struggle to make the respectable choice. This was one of hers. She resisted the true, honorable path and wrestled with all that what was good. Now, she must yield to this truth, let it go, and move on with her life. That is going to be the tough part; much more difficult than having to admit her impediments to the wounded woman on the other end of the lie."

"First off, all of a sudden you are now innocent? I understand what you are saying. Yet, I would choose a different word."

"Okay, 'in the lives of *devoted, loving by-standards*. Are those much more suitable words, my brilliant scholar; almost-friend?"

"Yes. Besides, you and I both know there comes a time in our lives where innocence grows faint and we become people who blame their ridiculous choices on the fact that they are not to the age of accountability quite yet.

'In the midst of all of this chaos, in which you have become entwined, you also must recognize that these two people, who seem to have plotted the most evil scheme against you and your family, are not the only antagonists at fault here. I probably should not be telling you this at this time of the morning and in the state in which I first found you. Yet, you always ask me to be utterly honest, as honesty does not seem to exist in the world around you anymore. I assure you, this frankness will be appreciated some day, if not one minute from now."

"While it may bite to hear what is sincerely real, I must hear it. In return, I will be dreadfully honest with you. You must promise you will not leave me if I am completely unaffected and frighten you."

"A difficult promise, but as I have told you before, I will never leave you."

"This desperate need for you stems from the fact that I have never felt this kind of pain before. Earlier today, as I was trying my best to keep a cheery presence for the sake of the only genuinely-innocent one in all of this, I felt completely broken.

'The age-old cliché, 'it is as if someone literally tore my heart from my chest,' never made sense to me, as it always sounded so exaggerated and absurd, especially since I had never been faced with a near-death experience such as this. And, after hanging up the phone (which proudly I did not throw) with the person I once viewed as a wicked imposter, I literally felt a vast emptiness where my heart exists."

"What took place in this bizarre conversation between you and Bathsheba?

"First of all, if you liken her to such a character, then you are giving him the title of David. Be careful, you are supposed to be the rational one.

'She asked me if I wanted to hear all of the gory details. Because I lacked any sense of rationality in that moment, I agreed to hear about the criminal acts that took place while he was on his four-month hiatus from his family. She informed me about the first time they met, the first phone call, the first night out, the first sexual encounter, the trip to Tahoe, the first fight…and the many after that, the night she saw us together, the slap she lay to his face, and the breakup.

'There was no hiding it, this relationship existed and the intimacy, both physically and emotionally, tied these two people together, just as it once did me and him. I struggled to find any sense of peace. I begged and hysterically cried out for it; it was completely fruitless.

'For some reason, I feel as if I am supposed to endure this pain. This romantic idea, which I am oftentimes married to, is what has been keeping me from melting into this floor and covering myself up with the remnants of my sorrow."

"There is someone else in your life that needs you as well. She is watching your every move. How you handle this will affect how she handles pain, laughter, sorrow, rejection, and everything else that life puts in her path. You will endure this torture and she will be watching. Any soreness that stems from pure jealousy, the fear of loss, and the humility that accompanies the violation of a contract, will fade-if you allow it."

"The pressure seems absolutely inane sometimes; inhuman really. Who one earth is supposed to keep it all together through this crazy turbulence? Then I think of her and all of this seems so foolish. While I am sitting here on this maddening floor, she, in all of her resilience, is patiently waiting for me to heal and be of some worth. My frailty, which teaches her that people do suffer and come to roads in their lives that are painful, must eventually be won over by the vigor to fight through life's trepidations."

"It is when you actually represent this truth of yours that you will find peace."

"I promise tomorrow I will undergo a huge undertaking; I will attempt to put these words into practice. For I have always excelled in the art of talking and have always lacked the talent to put my philosophies into practice."

"This will be our new challenge. I will see you soon, my friend."

"Adieu."

The Sixth Night

Humility unraveled: the most painful
experience of a dear friend

*"The practice of peace and reconciliation is one of the
most vital and artistic of human actions."*
~Thich Nhat Hanh

"here are times in our lives when we feel so broken; shattered to the point where the constant sea of tears seems to be our only way of knowing if we still are truly alive. I can say, even though I have bathed in these very edifices of defeat, dejection, and loss, I have never been subjected to the kind of grief that turns someone inside out, forcing them to come face to face with what personifies the very depths of their soul-their raw, authentic self."

"*Your* soul seems to be completely in ruins tonight. Yet, judging from the tone of your voice, it must not be your own heart that is of concern to you right now."

"I cannot even truly explain what my heart feels. Yes, the past few months have been excruciatingly painful and I have, more than once, questioned the existence of love, passion, and wondered if either of them truly can exist between two people. Today, all of those thoughts, emotions, and burning issues were completely immobilized by a shocking, horrific phone call that seemed to be one peculiar, outrageous joke played on a very dear friend.

'I was going about my day, busying myself with the tedious activities that so often engulf my existence, when my phone rang.

'My mother, whose voice is usually soft and filled with a mellifluous joy that always acts as a source of my daily therapy, was on the other side of the phone. Because her tone was much more hysterical and anxious than what I am used to, I knew there was something awfully wrong.

'It's Judy,' she cried.

'At that moment, I knew my dear friend Judy, whose short life has already been filled with more agony than most people can handle, had just been inflicted with the most destructive wound that has utterly shattered people's souls.

'For years she fought against all of life's misgivings with a grace that could not help but inspire those around her. She has been plagued by many losses, and now, at the age of twenty-two, when she has finally found peace, life tortures her yet again. This time, I am not sure where she will find the strength to fight this heartache.'

"Where has this angst stemmed from?"

"Two years ago, Judy moved to Hawaii to help take care of my niece, Katie. It was there that she met the man she wanted to spend her life with-Derek. He was stationed on the main island as a sergeant in the Army. After spending time with him, Judy knew she had met someone who would continually love her for everything that embodied her as a woman; her resilience, compassion, independence, even her quarks."

"What happened?"

"Their marriage, their colorful life together, which was supposed to beautifully commence in October, just came to a devastating halt this morning. Now, instead of planning her dream wedding, she will plan his funeral.

'You see, Derek was stationed in Iraq for the past four months. It was there that he would write Judy many letters, sing her songs over the telephone, and become an inspiration to the many disheartened men in his company who desired to be home with their loved ones."

"Had you met him?"

"Once. He was a funny red-head who had a contagious fervor for life, a fantastic sense of humor and an illustrious enthusiasm for fashion. As we sat there eating pizza, I listened to his commentaries on a war that I realized I knew little of. He was getting ready to begin his tour in a couple of weeks, yet the fear that I envisioned would accompany someone getting ready to face the relentless enemy head-on, was absent. My meeting with him was both mystic and humbling. His vehemence to follow through with a treatise he made at such a young age, whether he believed in it or not, was astounding. While I have met men and women who so zealously fight for our freedom, there was something in his eyes that spoke of passion. This passion did not seem to only exist for Judy, or for his promise, but for life.

'Now, he is gone. I just do not understand why people so full of love, compassion, and everything that is good are taken from us? How is Judy going to get through this heartache? How will she ever spend one moment not facing a despair that sends some people into irreparable states of madness? How will she breathe?"

"She just will."

"Promise?"

"I have only ever made one promise to you-I will never fall short in loving you, or anyone else for that matter."

"Why is so difficult for humans to love so deeply, as you do? I know that at this moment in my life, I should not make such harsh statements, as I am jaded to any true idea of what it is to value someone. Yet, I have always been haunted by this fear that I will never unreservedly love."

"Are you fearful that you will never be loved?"

"I used to become anxious when I thought that any form of love I would receive would be provisional. Now, what I fear most is that I will never be able to shower someone with the type of love that is unrestricted, real, the epitome of beauty. I want more than anything to become utterly vulnerable to the point where my love for someone encompasses more than myself."

"I believe your great Artist once implied that to love is the greatest gift of all. Is this your dream?"

"Most assuredly. I do know that I must first work on those fears and vices that have become plastered on my heart before I am able to free the very edifice of love from its haunting constraints."

"What one vice troubles you most?"

"My lack of humility. You see, when I first found out Derek had been stolen from those who loved him most, I was overwhelmed with anger. I then became conquered by sadness for his family and Judy and stood immersed in this incensed world for many hours. I have never been very good at understanding this whole side of the human condition; grief."

"It is something that everyone must face."

"While I am in tune with that reality, I still cannot confront it head on and come to grips with this world that makes no sense to me at all."

"Are you sure this is why you are angry?"

"Yes. This misery that so many people are plagued with every second is very real. That is enough to send someone into a dejected state of depression."

"I do believe this is where your sadness stems. I would never take that away from you. And still, I argue that there is much more to this new revelation of the human condition that is leading you to such a state of madness."

"If I really search the depths of my soul, as I have been trying so ardently to do lately, and if I am honest with myself, I will reveal to you why I am so disheartened with myself.

'In the midst of this war, all of the loss, tearing emotions, wrenching heart-ache, I have become immersed in my own sadness. People love to reiterate the fact that it is all relative. I even gave in to this notion once, maybe twice for that matter. I have recently concluded, especially after witnessing the kind of pain that stole my dear friend's heart from her body, that it is, in fact, not all relative."

"Are you sure you do not want to retract that statement?"

"Most certainly. Whoever said divorce is like death must be absolutely crazed. For these past few months, I too became disillusioned by this ideology that to walk through the trepidations of divorce is much like losing someone to death. After witnessing such pain as Judy has unjustly become inflicted with, I have quickly realized that it is entirely unfair to even remotely compare the two.

'While through my divorce there have been moments when I have said to myself that I had no choice in the matter, I actually did. I made the choice to leave and to follow through with the severance of my marriage. I have heard it argued that for some who are faced with divorce, no choice was made; it was forced on them just as death is thrust onto others. While this may be true, there is a certain level of pain that cannot even touch the unjust realms of death.

'Judy had no say in the matter. The person she loved and prayed would cherish her forever was taken from her in one moment. No chance to say goodbye, no final embrace, no last laugh from the man she loves so passionately."

"Does it frighten you that you can change your ideas so quickly, especially on so crucial a matter?"

"It is such a liberating feeling when all that you have held to be true is quickly turned in to the most ridiculous farce that has plagued your mind. This revelation that your heart knows a new truth is quite cathartic."

"Are you sure it does not frighten you?"

"Of course it does. As a prideful human being, I would love to believe that this constant fear, which abounds in these times of pandemonium, does not ever absorb itself into the very core of my existence. In turn, I would love to say that I am scared of nothing. I am not scared of being shaken. I am not scared of divorce. I am not scared of death.

"Instead, I cry whenever I realize that I have little control of these ideas that consume everyone's lives at some point or another. Some call me a control freak because of this reality. Maybe so. Yet, I believe that if we all searched our souls, we would find that this fear abides in all of us, just in different forms and on different levels."

'What does frighten me most is the sudden realization of my inability to be humble at certain points in my life. I became awakened to this lack of humility the night that I lay on floor in tears because I did not know how I was going to get through this divorce. Judy, whose soul was in pieces in the next room over, was alone and I was thinking only of myself and my sad situation. She needed me and I gave my thoughts, my time, my heart only to myself."

"What will you do now that your heart has become aroused to the fact that this vice, which C.S. Lewis calls the father of all sins, has played such a significant role in your life?"

"I would love to say that I will change and that when I wake up tomorrow, I will be a better person. Yet, being the realist that I am (if I could only be a raging romantic…), I know that this will not transpire at exactly 6 o'clock a.m. on Monday morning. It will take much time to repair who I have become."

"And Judy?"

"Just as you have done for me, I will listen to her, embrace her, and be her friend; her silent friend when I need to be, and her loving, insightful friend when she asks."

"I am always there for her too."

"My heart would believe no differently. Good night."

"I will tell her you say good night as well."

"Thank you."

The Seventh Night

The rapture of an imperfect union

*"It is not a lack of love, but a lack of friendship
that makes unhappy marriages."*
~Friedrich Nietzsche

"*O*h, hello. What are you doing here? I need to sleep; not converse with some unseen rational being that obviously thinks he, or she, has all the answers. Such a thing is most certainly the opposite of rational; it is totally ridiculous to think the answers are within anyone's grasp."

"Wow, you must have had quite the week. You have never been so cold and angry with me. I will excuse a friend's nasty behavior on account of the fact that she is not completely sane right now. But, please try to be a little more cordial. I am only here to help you."

"I am so sorry. This week has been filled with turbulence, an unreasonable outcry of tears, and a chilling bitterness that I did not believe I was capable of. I hate to compare myself to a tragic hero, but I finally understand what Julius felt when Brutus struck him with the fatal stab. He was completely blind sighted; unaware that his most loyal friend would conspire against him. Sadly, I don't think my foe has the kind of conscious that will eat at him and cause him to find any fault in what he has done. He will most likely not take a sword and thrust it into himself out of guilt. Thank goodness poetic justice is almost always served."

"Is that what you really want; for his life to be reduced to rubble as well? It seems as though that Artist you so often call upon advises that you turn the other cheek and love unconditionally, even those who break vows and find comfort in lying, cheating, and stealing. I doubt that you would find joy in the damnation of a loved one, past or present."

"It is not that I want to see him suffer; well, maybe just a little bit if I am going to be completely honest with myself, and you for that matter. I am having a very difficult time grappling with the theory that no effort was placed on his part in fixing this crazy union. Was I really that easy to let go of? Am I just some passerby who was sent on a quest to fill a void in his life for a moment? If so, I don't understand why the mission was not one of those stealthy, short-lived, Tom Cruise ones? They always make it look so easy.

'I walked around all day feeling like a disposable razor; one inexpensive Bic in the midst of a million others. He would use me for a time, and then move onto the next one until she too lacked whatever it was that made him feel larger than life."

"Was today the day? Is this the reason you are likening yourself to a toiletry. You could at least think of yourself as one of the more luxurious types, like a Venus."

"I am so glad you are finding the humor in all of this. By the way, I would not associate me with a love goddess. I also have failed miserably in the love department."

"Just because your marriage was not a success does not mean you fall short when it comes to love. Love is not measured by winnings and failings. Love truly triumphs when you allow yourself to become vulnerable, not fearing what the future holds. You, my friend, would have laid down your life for this person. Do you not believe that is love?"

"What you are revealing does make sense. Yet, I feel like such a failure. I woke up this morning a wife, tonight I am a divorcee."

"Don't you see that you were so much more than a wife? While this was most definitely a part of you, it was not the essence of you."

"I constantly wrestle with this truth. I know that there has always been so much more to me than being a wife. I just have continually been utterly unsure about how to be the woman I truly am and his wife at the same time. These two never seemed to coexist. Their worlds would never have survived."

"Are you sure?"

"Some days I am; some I am not. I suppose fear of failure has kept my real self under the surface."

"I do not mean to pry, but would it help to discuss what happened today?"

"I always try to embrace every day, knowing that each breath I take is such a perfect blessing; that each sunset a renewal, each sunrise a new beginning. Today was entirely different. My perceptions on everything seemed distorted.

'My alarm, who was my worse enemy this morning, before the final hearing at least, rudely screamed at me at 5 a.m. Remember, I have not had to get up this early in three years. I cannot believe this was the day to begin another new journey at such a god-awful time in the morning."

"Was today your first day back in the classroom?"

"Oh, yes. I was supposed to get up, have a wholesome breakfast, get Ami ready for her first day of preschool, walk into my new classroom, and prepare to move in all of my enthusiastic learners a newfound love of the arts. How I was supposed to do all of this in the midst of an irrevocable ending to a marriage that was supposed to conclude at 11 a.m., was outside of my comprehension. Nonetheless, I prepared for the daunting task ahead of me.

'Remember, this is all a blur, as it most assuredly had to be in order to survive D-Day.

'I dropped my precious little girl off at preschool; her first, frightening, guilt-ridden day (for me at least, the horrible mom who had to go back to work full time and leave her child in the abyss of strangers-another issue to be discussed some other time. This self-deprecation is yet to be shaken).

'I then arrived at school; rosters, novels, lesson plans, behavior plans, syllabi, smile, false sanity in hand. After greeting the tenured teachers and administrators with a confident air looming about me, I neared the ravine that I most definitely was going to plummet down before the end of the day.

'The bell, which I have been frightened of over the past week, rang and I lectured to my impressionable scholars who were all, for the moment, amendable to the rules I had set before them. They must have read the terrified look on my face and acquiesced out of the sheer horror that this crazy lady, who used to be a Mrs., was going to be in control of their fate for the next school year. They also must have been seeking atonement for the way they treated the teacher before me.

'As my next period, which seemed to last forever, drew to a close, my substitute for the next hour-and-a-half, casually strolled through the door. He had no clue why I needed his earnest assistance. As if it wasn't enough that I had to face the daunting task of my first day back of teaching high school students, I had to walk the dreaded steps of judgment and face the lady in black.

'With an anxiety I had never felt before, I ran through the courthouse doors, only to realize it was just me, my new friend Hal (I never thought I would think of an attorney as such, but I do), the stoic assistant, and the judge who held my fate in her custody. The terrifying crowd that always filled the room was absent for once. At least something went right in the midst of this mayhem.

'The judge, who had a kind, understanding aura about her, calmed my spirits for the moment. For the next twenty minutes, I gave my oath that what I was saying was true and correct. The question that kept ringing through the muddled mind of mine was how on earth could this woman believe that I was not severing this oath of honesty as I was, at that very moment, breaking another vow that, four years ago, I promised to uphold?

"Where was he?"

"Absent. I must say, it is so humiliating to go to a final divorce hearing alone. My other half, as some would call him, did not even care enough about our marriage to be there when it was terminated. What a bizarre close to a chaotic, detached relationship."

"You had to go back to school I take it. No going home, drinking two bottles of wine, and drowning in your self-pity?"

"Hey, watch it. I assure you I would have ran, because that is what I do when faced with anything even remotely painful, and then I would have maybe had one bottle of wine to drink; not two. What do you think I am?"

"A woman who just lost her life partner and now needs to escape from the agonizing drudges of existence. That is all. I am not questioning your character; just trying to get to the juice of it all. No punt intended."

"Thank you so much for taking pleasure in all of this.

'Upon hearing the words 'dissolution granted', I had the strangest sensation tear at my heart. That conviction, which was always unwavering, eased and a peace filled me to the very core of my being. I knew, for once, that this decision to leave and start a new life, either alone or with someone new some day, was okay. While there was nothing euphoric or gratifying about it, as some people experience, I did not leave feeling utterly dejected and disheartened.

'Walking down the steps of judgment, which hopefully I will never have to step foot upon again, I felt much more relaxed than I anticipated. Yet, my heart still felt broken. I entered bearing one name, and I left with another. While there were many tribulations in my marriage, I cannot say delight did not encompass it as well. There were days full of pleasure and silent understanding between the two of us that will always satiate my memory.

'Sadly, these piercing, lovely reminiscences will always be just that, memoirs of a love lost."

"I would not say 'love lost', as I hold in all of my convictions that once loved, it can never vanish. It may not be the kind of love between a husband and wife, but it is love nonetheless."

"I am not sure I am following."

"Sometimes, people come into our lives to help awaken us to who we are, or who they are for that matter. The important aspects of us may have otherwise gone unseen. We love them wholeheartedly, invest our time, emotions, and passion in them and then they leave. This may seem entirely unfair and unreasonable, but there is nothing that you are not resilient enough to endure. You have learned so much about yourself: How you handle pain, what makes your heart become elated, at what point do you humble yourself and let someone else be the victor."

"I wish you had been with me when I first walked in, left the palace of doom, and went back to school to humbly teach those who depended on me to be their reasonable guide."

"I was with you all along. Someday you will realize that I never leave."

"As always, I went throughout my day, pretending my emotions, my heart, and my head were not all scattered about. I should have evaded all sense of responsibility, resorted to my fetal position, and bawled my eyes out the rest of the day. This probably would have been quite therapeutic.

'Instead, I hurried to my classroom, facing yet another new group of novice sophomores, and put on my finest game face. I am sure they discerned my brokenness from the onset of our discussion, as nearly all of their eyes were full of sympathy and a kindness that surpassed my understanding. Were they in the courthouse with me when my marriage was terminated by the declaration of two words? Did they sense my fear, my dejection, my failure and therefore grant me, their vulnerable new teacher, clemency for the time being?

'Whether this careful concern was premeditated or not, I cannot be certain. I do know it gave me the greatest faith in humanity, which I desperately needed at that moment. As I looked into the faces of all thirty-four of my new apprentices, I had a lasting epiphany. These young adults, who society so often leaves behind on account of the fact that they are too corrupted to teach, will help ameliorate this pain. While many of them know little of marriage, some have unwillingly become experts in brokenness."

"Yes, suffering, which is universal, may undergo an attack using different weapons. While you may turn to a great glass of wine, a pen, and paper, and then fall on your knees in desperation, others may find comfort in tears and words. Some even find it necessary to become completely anesthetized to their reality."

"But why is suffering so necessary? Why do we get to the place where the only sensation that seems comforting is deadened? Is it unequivocally imperative that I feel downright damaged?"

"Yes."

"Oh, that is reassuring."

"For in these moments of defeat, who we really are is aroused and our greatest sense of self emerges. It is impossible to find the absolute joy in life without first recognizing the eerie sensation that pain instills in us."

"Thank you for your great discourse on suffering."

"You are welcome. Dare I ask what the rest of your day entailed?"

"There were tears, many of them."

"And wine."

"That too."

"You will find that the former will dwindle. As far as the latter, with that I also am not equipped to help with."

"Good night, my muse."

"Good night, Ms."

The Eighth Night

Passions unraveled

*"I believe that we are solely responsible for our choices,
and we have to accept the consequences of every deed,
word, and thought throughout our lifetime."*
~Elisabeth Kubler-Ross

"**W**here are you? I know I have seemed distant over the past few weeks, but again, I need you. I truly believed I was finally headed down the path of sanity, when an inspiring someone timidly strolled into my life. My nights have been satiated with laughter, wonder, contentment, and assurance that this heart, which was once shattered, is finally going to experience a major renovation. While I am the foreman in this colossal renewal, I finally realized there is someone much greater than me who delights in this type of business and who is much better suited for the task. I could not help but to be elated upon this epiphany.

'Then, in my nonsensical moment of weakness, I started to unravel what the great Artist has begun to repair; the essential human article that has been His specialty for many, many years. Silently, I yielded to a proposal that was not only completely absurd, but utterly precarious. Because it clashed with the moral upbringing I always endeavored to uphold, I was fated to endure the repercussions of this scandal tenfold. This acquiescence would haunt me for years to come, I assure you."

"I knew you would need me eventually, but the severe language you are throwing out there leads me to believe that my vacation is not going to be nearly as long this time."

"The mere reality that I have once again forsaken the Supervisor in this ongoing plan to continually fill my heart with an excess of peace, is enough to create in me another era of madness of the most epic proportions."

"A little dramatic I'd say."

"Please sit back and brace yourself for the story you are about to hear. You might want to cozy up to the seat on the floor you have become so accustomed to over the past eight months.

'I truly was, for once, minding my own business when this charming, strikingly-attractive gentleman, whom I had not seen for a number of years, just came strolling through the door. My nerves, which always get the best of me and send me into quite a frenzy, took charge and my words were sauntering about, creating the kind of gibberish that reverberates throughout the preschool classrooms of America; not from the mouth of an educated, twenty-something whose profession it is to teach 200 knowledge-hungry teenagers how to speak proper English. Wow, are they in for a treat.

'Upon witnessing the sheer beauty that epitomized this acquaintance of mine, I suddenly became enveloped in the most passionate love scene I could design to fit within the realm of my imagination. Remember, I lack experience in this whole sexual field of study. Nonetheless, as he was standing there talking to me, our steamy love-making session was running through my mind; not one racy detail being left out. I could feel his bronze, vigorous abs, which I must admit were reminiscent of Brad's Achilles in Troy, blending into my body. My God, I was starting to feel the heat wave steaming its way through my skin.

'His refined words and eloquent dissertation on life were enough to draw me deeper into this fairytale I was so-ardently creating. I struggled to maintain my composure while the blameless victim stood there as I, the young temptress, unconsciously made a fervent attempt to entice him with my heated eyes.

'Then, that horrible hue of red that robs my so-called painted layers, surfaced and I succumbed to the coy adolescent that I apparently never released as I became an adult. Much of me eventually matured, yet I never did nurture the bold, confident part of me when it comes to conversing with those of the opposite sex. So, there I stood-mimicking the very essence of the young adults I was teaching.

'If he had any suspicion I was undressing him as he stood there, he most likely would have run in the other direction. I finally averted my eyes, regained my composure, consulted with my mature self for a moment, and began speaking. This poor man had no clue he was actually having a monologue, as I was far removed from anything he was actually saying the past five minutes of our conversation.

'For days, my mind would not let go of all of the divine details that encompassed this man. I would find myself daydreaming about days on the beach, wrapped in the ever-forgiving, miraculous sunset, drinking wine, discussing Nietzsche, Dostoevsky, St. Exupery, and even Seuss, creating beautiful treatises on life out of any subject. The man I had envisaged for years was finally in reach."

"And you are lying here depressed because…"

"He will be my muse that I must visualize only in my dreams. His life is already full and I would only disrupt the peace that always seems to trail behind him wherever he moves."

"From the look on your face, I can see that your prince charming did not only surface in your dreams, as you stated he would."

'Well, I did not stop at that realization. Out of sheer passion and an inability to control my wild desires, I ignored all reason and my blushing stories began to develop into a reality."

"Why have you not told me of this? What is the reason for your absence over the past few weeks?"

"I would love to say conviction, guilt, not owning up to my poor decisions. But, the answer does not rest in what should be obvious. I have been on a whirlwind of the most passionate, extraordinary kind. This woman, who has never fulfilled her wildest fantasies, is having the most difficult time disregarding the fact that she has never been so utterly attracted, both physically and intellectually, to this person who draws out in her such raw feelings."

"How did this begin?"

"It is all Kierkegaard's fault. As I look back on it, I realize what a paradox it all was. As we were sitting there discussing what we loved most about Kierkegaard's eloquent story about Abraham's humility and sacrifice, we were unconsciously laying the foundation for an affair that would be destined to end in loss."

"Unconsciously, huh? You sure?"

"No, of course I am not. That is why you are here.

'We discussed the great question of humanity: Does one live with passion alone or should reason be our guide? My god, why on earth haven't one of those great, brilliant philosophers made enough sense to give me a straightforward answer that is unequivocally right on point? I would love it if they could stamp the truth on my heart so that I did not waver on one of the most crucial questions to ponder as one precariously drifts through life.

'Over the next couple weeks, we exchanged adoring glances, beautifully-written notes demonstrating our newfound, burning affection, secretive meetings and unspoken bouts of silence that seemed to strengthen our desire for one another. While we were incredibly restrained at first, our once-muted longing to become absorbed in each other's grasp took hold of us.

'I tried so hard not to become engrossed in an affair that I knew was absurd and was most certainly not capable of going anywhere. Yet, when he asked me to innocently embrace him upon his departure I could not resist the unaffected feelings that invaded my mind. I was hoping, for the sake of reason, that when we touched, the ardent, physical passion would not exist; that what we had was a pure, rare friendship where two people truly understood the convictions and zeal for truth that overwhelmed their souls every day.

'I was exceedingly wrong.

"What we had was much more than just some simple meetings of the minds. We found something in one another that people really do search for their entire lives."

"So, what is the problem?"

"While I am wholeheartedly alone, he is not."

"Oh, that is a huge problem. Especially considering the fact that most of the time you want to eviscerate the man who threw you to the trenches in order to start a life with a new woman. That is quite the contradiction. I surely do hope you have been grappling over this these past few weeks."

"At first, no. While it may seem frightening to you, I have been in a rapturous state of mind ever since I first saw him. Now, after a few days of feeling his embrace and experiencing his enthusiasm for everything that I believe to be real and true, I find myself in the midst of a pandemonium that I cannot calm. Last week, after sitting down for hours, I tried inventing phrases that would convince him what we had was a whimsical affair that was both reckless and insensitive. Before we completely gave into our sexual passions, we needed to end this. The damage was only going to get worse, and it truly is not within the bounds of either of our characters to give into such hasty behaviors. We both have been told to put others above ourselves, and this was definitely quite the opposite. As I put my heart to pen, what I created was:

My friend,

I'm not quite sure words can truly tell the story of my heart right now. Yet, I will try with all of my soul to be naked and true in all of my thoughts and desires. I will start by saying that I have been, for the first time in my life, really touched by a man who seems perfectly raw, yet so real to me. For that, I am eternally blessed and shaken. I tell myself to hold back and to live rationally, for my very thoughts that have overwhelmed me my whole life have been to be good, to put others before myself, and to love wholeheartedly, sacrificing my own happiness for those who pretend to exist. While I have fought with my whole self as to whether I truly believe in goodness and sacrifice, I have never once questioned the unaffected, genuine existence of love. I know that I have never really stared it in the face, but I always knew I would be wildly touched by it some day. How do I avert my eyes, and worse my heart? For a goodness that I really don't know we are really capable of? It is as if I am fighting for a cause that I don't know is worth fighting for. It would be unjustifiable to let go. I think of one of my favorite poems, "When love beckons to you, follow him, though his ways are hard and steep." I have never questioned those words, and I'm not sure why I question them so deeply now. You have reached the deepest layer of me that no one has even come close to-I cannot deny that with one small part of my soul.

I was hoping to be the better person and to make the impossible decision to mold my feelings into a false reality, to pretend our passion and our delicate thoughts and embraces were a figment of my heart's imagination. For that is what you asked of me. I say to you that I cannot embrace an idea that is false. That would interrupt the core of my being. I apologize that I could not be the better person and walk away from someone who has shown me for the first time what it is to be truly touched and what it is to have my mind and heart stirred in ways that make me feel alive.

I believe our mantra has become: "Within you I lose myself. Without you I find myself wanting to become lost again." I leave you with those words and hope that you will see either the beauty in them or the destruction. While the paradox is frightening, it is a decision and a question that has been pondered by thousands. We are among those and it is our choice as to which road to take. My mind says, take the higher. Yet, my heart says, how often do we feel someone's face and really become a part of their existence-their beautiful, untouched, absolute existence? I have asked myself is absence truly the only cure to love. I'm not quite sure I can justify this statement, as it seems like our passions would become intensified and our pull to each other would break the core of our beings.

This decision can truly only be yours. I cannot make it and I will stay away, still stirred and touched, if that is our fate. I ask that you will know, every time you look at me, that your eyes also have become deeply embedded in the deepest parts of my soul.

"Tell me you did not give this to him."

"I did, and it did not quench the thirst we had for one another. We became more immersed in our relationship. Our caution, which used to follow us wherever we went, was completely obstructed by the attraction that seemed to build every time we crossed paths.

'Today, we realized the road we were so dangerously strolling down would only lead to heartache; not of our own, but of those we love. We grappled with the whole idea of passion. Why would God create such a beautiful gift and then take it from us because of the whole legalistic idea of good versus bad? Who created such an outlandish idea anyway, the Puritans? They really knew how to twist and turn the words of an Artist and make Him into something that He cannot possibly be? Whether or not we were committing sins of the worse kind-putting ourselves above others and committing adultery-at this moment, neither of us can answer."

"You do not give yourself enough credit. The answer, which may not be evident to everyone, lies at the core of your convictions. Your heart, which has always escorted you to different places in your life, may not always be the best guide, as your favorite author once argued. It is when you turn inside out, become entirely raw and feel completely helpless; that is where you find your answers. You, my friend, are not there yet, as this pain you have experienced over the past year has concealed your thoughts, therefore tarnishing any sense of that which is real for you. The relationship between you and your muse brought you to this point. While you may have ended something that made your heart feel elated, you have become one step closer to finding the person who lies underneath the woman you have hidden from the world; under the surface that you have never allowed people to delve into."

"What about this aching pain that I cannot extinguish?"

"It too will fade, just as it slowly has over the past months we have shared."

"Promise."

"I will be here until it does. Good night."

The Ninth Night

She comes unleashed

"Do as the heavens have done, forget your evil;
With them forgive yourself."
~William Shakespeare

"**I** didn't even have to beckon you tonight. I am going to assume you saw the look on my face this morning and immediately ran to my rescue. I will confess I pray you were on sabbatical yesterday evening when I unraveled all of my convictions, morals, and sense of self in order to quench a desire I have been holding in for months."

"From the sound of it, you need more than a rational mind to discuss the chain of events that took place. I will admit I am not well-versed in the whole priest trade. Please do not expect this to be the meeting of two out-of-character people; one being the person who must confess and the other to merely sit back, listen, and give his holy advice. If it is, I will see my way out of this feral place. Besides, from the tone of your voice, I can tell that we will need to devote much more time than usual if you are going to be repenting."

"Thank you, my smart-ass friend. You do speak some truth though. We might need hours to dissect my behaviors that came from a woman who swore she would never play the leading role in such preposterous activities."

"What did you do, call someone a bad name?"

"Oh no, it gets quite worse. When I tell you this story, please remember that I am one who has never invited drama into her life. I even blush when I have to walk into a room late and all eyes are on the lackadaisical individual who so rudely interrupted everyone's train of thought. How I ended up…dear goodness, I cannot even say where without turning the most frightening hue of red."

"You promised you would always adhere to the truth and admit all of your blemishes to me. This is the only way we can get through this crazy debacle together. Besides, it could not have been that bad. Were you unleashing from the most recent loss incurred in your life?"

"I am trying to find the humor in all of this, yet I am having a difficult time considering I am officially completely defected now; a tarnished divorcee whose imperfections are going to be divulged all across this peculiar town. I also have a person in my life who will always remind me of this blemish."

"Start from the beginning, leaving out only the futile details, as we do not have much time."

"I was tired. Tired of being the responsible one; dealing with the haunting, merciless creditors, getting up at 5 o'clock every morning to carry on my responsibilities as a mature, reliable adult, doing dishes, paying bills, folding laundry, dealing with incessant phone calls from *him*, blah, blah, blah. Oh, I cannot forget about the hours I must spend sinking into the poor pit of despair in order to emerge into a whole being again. In the midst of feeling ridiculously sorry for myself, I made the conscious decision to 'let it all go'."

"Conscious, hah?"

"Oh yes, I cannot even think about blaming this on anyone else. I woke up and told myself that I was going to rip off all of my virtuous layers and convert to a fanatical, outlandish semi-human being with not a care in the world. Maybe this would really cure my obstruction of reality for a moment? Or, maybe it would make it worse? Whether the answer lies in the former or latter, I still am not completely sure. Like they say though, there are always consequences, seen or unseen, heard or unheard; they are always there. I do know I will not be able to hide from these nonsensical decisions for a long time to come.

'I remember it all, most if it anyway, very clearly. It started as an innocent evening of friends at the local wine bar. My first-rate, dear friend Michaela, great wine, fine conversation, heavenly brie cheese (The Artist really knew what he was doing when he created the delectable ingredients for this luxurious victual), an adorable waiter, and perfect shoes. The night was faultless.

'Then, he walked in the door. The man my friends had been wanting me to meet. Of course, I did the only thing I know how to do at the ripe age of 27. I shook his hand, turned that awful, scarlet shade that matched the letter that, if I had any conviction, should be permanently pasted to my breast, and turned my head in the other direction. It should be of no surprise to you that I have been single for a year and have yet to go on a date or converse with someone from the opposite sex who might even be remotely interested in courting me."

"Wow that was quite the evening."

"Oh no, it does not stop there. You see, the perfect Artist also created this juice that He discusses in his novel quite frequently. Sadly,

I took it to another level. Apparently, I forgot to read those other words that rest between 'they drank wine' and 'thou shall not'.

'After a few glasses of Columbia's best grape juice, I regained the gumption that only creates itself when my true character is raptured from my body and some other insane person takes its place."

"Wait a second! You don't really believe that this is not just some version of you that is terrified of surfacing because you fear what others will think of you if you are completely honest and real?"

"Do you want to hear the story or not?"

"You may continue miss-I-don't-want-to-deal-with-reality."

"After a few drinks, I felt as if I had triumphed over my inhibited, timid self and turned into this gregarious, unreserved socialite who was ready to face my prince charming straight on. Now, I know that this may not seem like a feat for most people, but you must remember that I have never dated and my ex-betrothed is the only person I have ever been with. So, be patient as I tell my tale.

'While I was completely careless the rest of the night, I must admit it felt refreshing to finally get out and not feel so downright sad about what was going on around me. I had great discussions, met some very kind people, and ended up reliving my Europe experience; walking barefoot in the dark, trying to make my way home. Only this time, instead of strolling down the cobblestone alleyways of Venice with my cherished friend Rebekah, I was sauntering through the pothole-ridden, unevenly paved streets of Sonora with this attractive, liberal prince-charming I was destined to meet in this small, god-forsaken parish. It wasn't Venice, but it was romantic nonetheless.

'We finally made it home and, for the sake of time, I will leave out the next few hours."

"Well, what was so wrong with your evening, other than the fact that you became ridiculously inebriated and commingled with some very enlightening, compassionate people?"

"This is the part where I find myself completely confused. While I remember quenching that thirst that has tormented me for months, I am ashamedly conflicted about it. Why do I not feel guilty? Why did I wake up and feel the most mesmerizing, pleasurable sensation? What happened to the convictions that have always ruled my being? Who in the heck is this preposterous fugitive who could only think, 'why on earth have I been so deprived my whole life?'"

"Oh. This is quite uncomfortable. I did not see our conversation turning in this direction. Please tell me this is at least going to be PG-13."

"Oh, no. I am not even sure we can rate this R. Since you are quite the conservative, I will omit the provocative, racy details."

"Thank you."

"Mêléeing over my sudden loss of conviction is not the only battle I am in the midst of right now. I have earned myself a spot on the front lines of the fiercest clash of the exes I could find myself. It was ugly this morning, and I know it is only going to get dreadfully worse.

'He, that person I cannot name, witnessed my lewd act first hand. While it is most certainly his fault that he became entangled in such an event, the fact remains that he saw his pure, unsullied ex-wife enfolded in the arms of someone who resembled Adam before his foolish wife decided to eat the dreaded apple."

"How did he get involved?"

"It's really quite outrageous, almost so that I still cannot believe it actually happened. My poor, innocent brother, who has been knocked out on pain medications for the past four days, was peacefully sleeping on my couch, when he heard a knock on my door. Not realizing that his virtuous sister had snuck into her own house at goodness-knows-what-time in the morning and had an unknown visitor, he walked to the door and let in the imposter.

'Now remember, one cannot paint this town red without every citizen hearing about it within the hour. I swear they put out special announcements on the town radio every time there is pressing news to be heard. That night, apparently I was breaking news. I got my fifteen minutes of fame, again.

'He thought he would show up to see if the headlines were genuine and if the evidence of my crime was accurate for once.

'There he stood, with all of his proud glory, in the doorway to my room. Upon turning on the lights, he walked to the end of his old bed, turned the covers, and there we were, me and the man whose first name I was only familiar with. I thought the whole room was going to collapse on top of me. It was already spinning. Why not just cave in already? That would have been nice.

'Eden most definitely sank to grief in that very moment. He looked at his face, then looked at me, and commanded my new friend to leave. His lack of control, as prince charming said no and pulled the blankets back over him, was priceless for a moment.

'His pride, which always seemed to be his closest friend, was reduced to nothing in those few, short minutes. While my, you-got-what-was-coming-to-you mentality existed for some hours, my humility took front stage as soon as I had time to relive the frightening encounter.

'First of all, it was entirely out of character for me to bring someone home. You would think I would have gotten that out of my system in college. I guess you could call me a late bloomer. Second, I have never been one to find delight in the anguish of others. Yet, if I am going to be honest, as I promised, I was thrilled that he witnessed something that would make his heart ache as mine did. This must sound completely cruel and you must twinge at the realization that you have had to actually comfort me, a callous, heartless villain who would make such mischief and delight in it."

"I actually am not shocked that you played such a role in such a dramatic short story. After all, as Hamlet once said to his beloved Ophelia, 'God gave you one face, yet you paint yourselves another'. Maybe your true face, your soul, is really not the one that everyone sees.

'I am neither appalled at such behavior. You have held it in for so long, to the point where that smile of yours sometimes is not even genuine; just a façade to keep the wolves from tearing at your heart."

"Why thank you for your candid response to such a humbling situation. I was traumatized an hour ago, and now I find myself completely shaken. Your compassion and understanding is absolutely remarkable right now. I think I am going to try to sleep on that now."

"The sarcasm, which equates phone throwing, has now become your forte? You might want to work on that."

"Will do, my acquaintance that really has no chance of becoming my friend after that comment."

"Good night. Oh, and any chance that prince charming of yours might be coming back? I will be surprised if he does."

"You always have such an abundance of encouragement seeping out of you."

"Watch that sarcasm. Remember, you become what you hate."

"Such luminous insight. I will sleep on that. Good night."

The Tenth Night

Pancakes at midnight

*"The Grand essentials of happiness are: something to do,
something to love, and something to hope for."*
~Allan K. Chalmers

"**I** have no need for you tonight. This irrationality feels absolutely fantastic and any invasion of the most perfect space is ridiculously unnecessary. Please allow my entire being to be saturated with my memory of last night."

"Then why are you sitting there, under that naturalist painting, at this hour of the morning? Pardon me, but usually you have surrendered to sheer insanity by the time I have reached you."

"I will step out of this haze and share this space with you I suppose.

'While I may seem completely elated from last night's events, I must avow that the overbearing psychotic part of me is still trying to come in first place and beat out any sense of euphoria that may have existed two seconds ago.

'As always, I am fighting with my dual personalities, perceptions, realities…whatever they may be. Hopefully some day you can help me reach some sort of conclusion as to who I am and what I actually believe to be true."

"Unfortunately that fight may never end."

"Peace, at last."

"I will say that I can help you attain some sense out of all of this though."

"I am going to need much more than my senses to guide me through all of this; we know where those lead me."

"True. But who is to say that where you are escorted will send you straight to that place of eternal damnation? Let's speak rationally here. Your entire aura is different tonight."

"I cannot ever understand why whenever I do something out of character I feel so extremely guilty. I had the most amazing time last night and here I am, elated one minute and shameful the next."

"What did you do, go out and commit a felony?"

"Worse, I had pancakes at midnight."

"You should most definitely be sent directly to absolute darkness for that misconduct. Please tell me they did not have bananas on them?"

"Actually, the pancakes, the bananas, *and* the aftermath of my midnight snack were especially succulent; I felt as though I was fifteen and after weeks of dreaming of my most perfect crush, I finally convinced him to notice me. And still, I am here feeling like I am going to need atonement the rest of my life for my selfish indulgence.

'You see, since I was fifteen, I have only dated one man, been married to one man, and have made love to only one man. That promise ring my mother gave me at age thirteen instilled in me a bit of conservative guilt. I knew if I ever 'gave myself' to someone else, I would have to be in penitence for the rest of my life. The thought of a one-night rendezvous was always entirely out of the question. That was for heathens who lived their lives as gypsies and harlots."

"Did your mother really instill this in you?"

"I have to admit that while she asked me to pledge my chastity, she has always been one to understand my intentions and love unconditionally. She just did not want me to be pregnant at seventeen-or fourteen for that matter.

'This really stems from my own distortion of my conservative upbringing."

"Then what is really behind the pancakes?"

"My new friend, who took part in the lewd act with me a couple of weeks ago, came over and we decided our stomachs needed some attention, as they were being left out by the constant meditation on other members of our anatomy.

'Being the non-cook that I am, he said he wanted to make me pancakes."

"How were they?"

"Beautifully-created, as I would expect nothing less. I am not sure someone with such creativity in every other aspect of his life would be capable of failing at making the simplest feature on the all-American breakfast menu.

'We ate our pancakes and then went back to what we had been doing before our stomachs took front stage."

"You are leaving out quite the details."

"And there are plenty of them. Yet, being that I still blush when a man makes eye contact with me, I am not going to be able to share them with you."

"Did you commit the ultimate crime?"

"Let's just say I no longer wear the 'one man' sign on my chest anymore."

"My goodness, twenty-seven and only been with two men. You are right-you are most definitely up there with the worst of them."

"While you may mock my convictions and ridiculous philosophies, this still does not negate the fact that I cannot sleep and am, *again*, immersed in an absurd state of mind.

'Many people, especially in my ever-so-liberal 'X-generation', believe that a list of two is quite admirable. It is only when you approach 100 that you should evaluate your moral code and plagiarize a new set of values from someone whose list is closer to the shorter end of the spectrum.

'This theory has never worked for me. I told myself at the age of nine (when I had no clue about sex) that I would be with one man only and if my husband ever left, or worse case scenario, died, I would swear a life of chastity. I had no clue that at the old age of 27, while at my sexual peak, I would be alone and suffering the worse case of pent-up sexual tension imaginable.

'Then, out of nowhere, bolts in Mr. Experience. Am I really supposed to ask him to kindly walk away and forget I ever saw him? I am sorry, but after one slight touch, the highest grade of steel would not have been able to secure the protective lock on my chastity belt. There was no doubt his key was destined to perforate the strategically-assembled security code I placed on my sexual identity."

"Instead of brooding over what you did last night, I think we need to start with the fact that your guilt, which always alters your cheerful countenance, seems to direct everything you do. When are you going to realize that human beings are fallible and that the most critical ideology that you must not abstain from is that of love?"

"Are you suggesting that I just give away my love to every man whose expertise it is to physically please women?"

"Do you really believe that I would give you such advice?"

"I just do not know how to balance these opposing tenets. Do I just let go and re-evaluate everything I have held to be *truth*? Change my values? Become a nun?"

"You know how to balance. Do you not remember reading about Emil Sinclair? His guilt, conscience, shame, fear led to the pain he suffered along his ever-winding road to self awareness. You recently vowed that one of your wholehearted beliefs is that if life is not painful and occasionally filled with devastation, then no learning and self-discovery is attainable.

'This shame you feel for succumbing to your flesh is incredibly universal. Still, you must not live in the shadows of your convictions and mishaps. At certain times in our lives, temptations are meant to be wrestled with. If you happen to give into them, it is critical that you ask yourself where brooding over the indiscretion is going to lead you."

"Living in the shadows of my wrongdoings is far more exhausting than reevaluating what I hold to be true and where my attention should be exerted at this point in my life. I do know that my failures are necessary if I want to continually reflect on who I am and what I stand for. I just can't keep up with the current emissions of failure I have exhausted lately.

"Your ever-present ideology, where perfection must constantly be attained in order to conquer life's *darkness*, is a powerful cause for your depressing condition.

'While the realistic consequences of your actions may not have been at the forefront of your mind at the moment, your heart and fervor for life have not been changed by your so-called mishap. Redemption is constantly making his rounds around these parts of the continent all-to-often lately. Consequently, your heart has not been cut off from the faithfulness of this liberator."

"What happens if I crave pancakes again?"

"Whether you are tempted to eat the entire plate or merely skim the first layer, I assure you finding the difference between implied truth and real truth is the key ingredient to forgetting about the 700 calories that satiated your body and left you feeling both euphoric and desolate at the same time. Then again, it may also encourage you rethink your caloric intake."

"Do I have your permission to cut back and have low fat, whole wheat ones?"

"As long as you know, before you begrudge yourself with guilt or make a decision based on false premises, that your decision is unadulterated."

"Is there a chance I will wake up this morning with decision in hand-low cal or utter indulgence?"

"Not likely. Nevertheless, I do promise the more you seek out the unaffected truth, the greater chance you will have in not wavering when faced with life altering decisions."

"I will definitely read the labels, ingredients and precautions included."

"Great idea."

"When is it not?"

"Next time, we will work on humility."

"Goodnight Ms. Prynne."

"I am officially marked, aren't I?"

"Only by your conscience."

"My conscience can take no more. Goodnight."

The Eleventh Night

I am changing my name to Ms. Feeblecorn

*"Do not waste yourself in rejection, nor bark against
the bad, but chant the beauty of the good."*
~Ralph Waldo Emerson

"**Y**ou look absolutely divine tonight. Your skin tone is matching quite nicely with the opaque hue of the wall, which has apparently become your closest companion since guilt and misfortune started invading your personal space once again.

'You were quite ecstatic a few evenings ago from your masquerade with the pancake-maker. What has plunged you out of step three and into complete mayhem again? Do you realize you are messing with the order of reality here; it is outrageous to believe step three can come before step one."

"I have no last name."

"Great. You have officially become a madwoman."

"Really, all craziness aside, I have been up all night trying to decide what name fits best with 'Brianna': Smith, Kerry, Needham; I even thought of Fitzneiman.

'You know, I once thought of myself as a woman with at least a smidgen of quasi-creative instincts. I now realize I have another fault—absolutely no artistic capability. Apparently my grandmother, who painted the most beautiful nudes, refused to pass down her precious DNA to her granddaughter."

"Are your really crying over stick figures?"

"Not even close. I received yet another phone call today."

"A collector."

"Worse—my dad."

"Now that's harsh."

"My dad is not the problem; it was his tone and the fact that he was calling a family meeting. I must remind you that his ability to converse with another human being about anything serious is quite limited. Therefore, I knew it was something frighteningly critical. Since he married my mom when I was nine, we have had maybe two family gatherings where important matters were to be discussed.

'While my instincts told me it was going to throw all of us into utter chaos, my romantic, irrational person promised it was all going to be a gathering of like hearts trying to catch up on life's happenings."

"I am guessing your rational was right, yet again?"

"Would you feel better if you were right?"

"But, of course."

"You may gloat in the accuracy of your assumption."

"I will. Now tell me about the great meeting of the hearts."

"My brothers, little sister, and I all had an idea as to the purpose of 'the dinner', as mom and dad have clearly not been happy for some time. Therefore, we tried to prepare ourselves for the worse and hope that they were going to tell us they decided on artificial insemination."

"That sounds entirely absurd."

"To most I guess. Still, it made sense to us.

'My step-dad, who has no biological children of his own, decided during his imminent mid-life crises that instead of going out and getting a girlfriend, or a Porsche for that matter, he wanted more than anything to have a child of his own."

"Isn't this a man who refuses to change diapers or be around children for more than fifteen minutes?"

"Our thoughts exactly. Yet, being a proponent of change, I believed that maybe, just maybe, somewhere in the midst of that stubborn, manly ego dwells a soft-hearted, patient, diaper-changing guru."

"When are you going to put your idealist views aside and cross over into the pragmatic side of life?"

"After this mishap in my nonsensical journey, I am not sure even the tiniest fragment of my romanticism will survive."

"You just may have to balance that naïve romanticism and harsh realism for some time in order to get through this stage in your life.

'You see, according to most of the people who embody your generation, everything should work itself out under your own timelines, rules, and theories. Goodness forbid you change your attitude on a particular principle or assumption for the slightest amount of time in order to make sense of a certain situation."

"When am I going to find the time to study this morose notion of realism, which is inevitably going to assist in the damnation of my whimsical character and lead me to the dark side?"

"At three o'clock every morning. Isn't that the time you crawl out of bed and inhabit that teeny corner of your room anyway?

'Instead of sulking over your depressing thoughts and realities, why don't you consume your mind with both classical and modern ideas on the two conflicting ideologies? You may find that realists, while often categorized as bleak and pessimistic, find the most joy in life because they are able to weed out what could happen and what is actually going to happen."

"Now you are asking me to undergo a complete transformation of character. Did the sudden wrinkles and the rapid increase in cortisone levels not do enough for you?"

"Not a change in character, but in the way you view the world and the situations that leak out of the misplaced manholes and flood your very existence—including your perceptions of yourself and the world around you. When tackling difficult situations, remember that you do not have to change your beliefs, values, and self for that matter; you just have to change the way in which you see and approach the world."

"Easy for you to say; you don't have to do anything but be entirely entertained by my mishaps and counsel me on how to fix these ridiculous failures."

"How is this 'failure' yours? Your father decided to leave, not you. This really has nothing to do with you. It is just really poor timing, which is most likely the reason you are carrying the burden inside your heart."

"Whenever I try not internalizing everything and make it my issue, I fail. While I do know this is his decision to abandon all of us, I still feel as though I am personally being attacked."

"First of all, you need to get over yourself. You are not the one being 'left'; your mother is. Second, no one has abandoned you—I am here, as I have always promised I would be. Your brothers and little sisters, who are grappling with the same pain and loss, are here too."

"I just do not know what life will be like without a father. Once he leaves, he will be gone. The slightest bit of communication may make its way through a phone line occasionally. Yet, I know he will find a young twenty-something and have some children of his own. As soon as his seed is planted, he will be off in some foreign field planning his future, not reflecting on his past. We will all be memories to be pondered when a certain scent or light passes by his senses. In time, he may not even remember how to recall where that certain memory stems from."

"He may leave you all behind. That does not mean you are fatherless."

"I will always have my Father and there is never a moment where I do not find serenity in that truth."

"Do you not have another father whose untamed enterprises brought you into this world?"

"Dear goodness. That will be the cause for another escapade with you at three o'clock in the morning."

"That bad?"

"I do love my 'real dad' very much. Most children have this inexorable forgiveness when it comes to his or her parents. I have always been such and never wavered when it came to my unconditional love for him.

'I know that while he was not always there and could not provide for me, he did love me the only way he knew how. Some say I am merely making excuses for his behavior. I say while his life has not always been a reflection of fatherhood, compassion, stability, responsibility, and kindness for that matter, he is still my father. This does not mean I have to welcome him into my own child's life when he is making certain decisions. Even then, his physical absence does not equate to a deficiency of spirit or love."

"Then why the sudden name-change to Feeblecorn?"

"My brothers, sister and I, who have had quite the number of name changes between the four of us, decided that it is time to start fresh and create a new name that would best suit us all. Joshua, my youngest brother, decided Feeblecorn was fitting for all of us."

"Brianna Feeblecorn. Sounds absolutely ravishing. Your students are going to love that one."

"It is better than Brianna Sannella-Willis isn't it?"

"No, just shorter."

"Thank you for your support."

"Are you not worried about the lady at the front desk?"

"Who might that be?"

"The lady with the big glasses, bloated hair, and raspy voice at the Social Security Administration's Office. She is going to ruin you with her one-full minute of disgorging laughter. Just stick with the simplest name you have ever had."

"Willis it is."

"You may get to change that one too…in time of course."

"Let's not even go there. My once-poor view of men has changed quite dramatically lately. The only view that saturates my mind is a dingy, impoverished, sordid landscape that is fit only for the heartless, cruel, dreadful human beings who dare inhabit such a setting."

"Poor Mr. More. If he only knew what you have done with his picturesque milieu. Do you not realize that it is sheer ignorance to lump an entire group of human beings together and create such a morbid picture?"

"Of course."

"Are you finished with your tangent?"

"I am tired of discussing this pain. I just want it all to go away and become a distant thought that I conjured up in my mind on some rainy day."

"The pain will be. The reality of what happened will not."

"May I excuse myself? I need to think about a name I will actually adopt."

"Just remember you are loved Ms. Willis."

"Underneath all of this, I know wholeheartedly that I am loved unconditionally and no divorce, separation, or even death can steal that from me. I just need to remind myself of this truth."

"You will, in time."

"Thank you for your faith."

"Thank you for your heart."

"Goodnight."

The Twelfth Night

First New Year's Eve out on the town

"There are as many nights as days, and the one is just as long as the other in the year's course. Even a happy life cannot be without a measure of darkness, and the work 'happy' would lose its meaning if it were not balanced by sadness."
~Carl Jung

"Each expression on your face always speaks a million words. You seem to have been completely demoralized, yet strangely that look in your eyes that usually accompanies such a depressing adjective, does not exist this morning. What have you been up to? Have you finally let all of your pain seep from your soul and tarnish the already-tainted atmosphere instead of your fragile heart?"

"I most certainly did. Now there are times in our lives when we wake up knowing our goal for the day, or week for that matter, is to make one crazy, rash decision after another. Yesterday was that day. In fact, the whole plot was entirely premeditated. I had eight hours to plan out the night, one wiled, untamed detail at a time. You see, I woke up at 4 o'clock the morning on New Year's Eve in my most favorite place in the world, San Diego. Why I did not make the seemingly obvious, rational decision to stay there and celebrate with my most sensible friends may seem crazy and outright unnatural.

'Yet, if I had, they would have loved me enough to keep their unruly, feral friend within the confines of a cultivated, docile place. I wanted to become immersed in the most dramatic form of disorderly conduct that I could imagine. I was ready to, for the first time, to give those Tuolumnites something to talk about. If they were going to discuss my life, my failures, and my quarks with each other, then I decided, since I was not entertaining enough before, to assist them in their neighborly conversations.

'So, I gathered my things and set out for small-town USA. I must say, it was the most ephemeral trip home, from San Diego at least, that I had ever experienced. That wild imagination of mine had me daydreaming about my immoral activities that would transpire in just a few hours."

"Do I dare ask for the racy details?"

"They are quite juicy, especially for my typically mundane life. Are you sure you are ready to see another side of me that only emerges on the rarest of occasions? This may be worse than that outlandish, out-of-character one-night-stand in which I played a significant role."

"I am not sure anything would surprise me at this point. We have been together for nearly a year and I feel as though I have seen it all;

well almost. Aside from murder in the first degree and a few other avant-garde affairs, your life has encompassed quite the plethora of some out-of-the-ordinary situations."

"I warned you. Now you, my new therapeutic sidekick, are going to have to listen attentively, whether you become nauseas or not.

'First of all, I was a bit sedated by the time I arrived at the scene of the crime. I had not slept and had outrageously drank a bottle of wine with my poor, innocent little brother, who has always had this view of me as an upright, model citizen. While he did witness my belligerence once at the good-ole Typhoon Saloon on my twenty-second birthday and then again this past Christmas Eve, he has never had to suffer through the inebriation of one convicted, old-school, wannabe harlot who never got out all of her gumption in college, Australia, or Europe for that matter.

"You could not have caused that much damage on such a festive evening."

"Oh, but I did. I am not sure the Rawhide has ever witnessed the likes of me, a self-proclaimed good girl gone bad? Over the next few days, people would ask me what happened to innocent Brianna Willis?"

"A little dramatic I'd say."

"It most certainly is. Yet, if you had been there to witness my gluttony of the mouth, you would have run in the opposite direction, never to counsel me again through my life's misgivings.

'Now, there was not going to be any running away from my past tonight. I was destined to run into *him* on this joyous occasion, as fate would not have it any other way."

"Was your meeting pleasant?"

"How could it be? It was to be the twelfth anniversary of our first date. Nothing pleasant was going to transpire from this meeting of two foes. I, as I so often do in a drunken stupor, yelled some hurtful, damaging words to the antagonist who has saturated my life with not-so-fond memories as of late. There was nothing else for him to do than leave.

'I then dangerously danced across the floor, attempting to lead the avid dancers who were much more sober than myself and therefore, were much better suited for the lead position (God forbid I actually allow a man to take charge). Also, according to unadulterated rumors from very reliable sources, I caused a fight between some just-as-ridiculous-as-me, inebriated buffoons. I was then bamboozled into thinking I had finally experienced pure bliss as my knight in shining armor fought off the foe who dare take our taxi."

"Please tell me you at least remember bringing in the New Years?"

"No, sadly I do not. Upon being cornered in the ladies room by two melodramatic nemeses, one blonde and one brunette, who felt compelled to discuss the recent happenings of both my ex-husband and my new fly-by-night romance, I decided to have yet another.

'Because my guardian angel is always armored with shield in hand, I did not suffer from any catastrophic mishaps that could have resulted from my outlandish behavior. I did, however, have to face my conscious head-on the next day as I struggled to make sense of the activities that took place the evening before. If they had not been so calculated, I may not have felt so guilty."

"You do know you are allowed to occasionally slip into a strange psychosis without having to rebuke yourself, right?"

"If I had not been so cruel and unkind to a man I vowed to respect and love the rest of my life, I may not have woken up feeling so dejected and guilty. Yet, the second he walked into that god-forsaken upheaval of a bar, I was determined to humiliate him for the pain he caused and turn his evening into a complete debacle."

"Did you finally make it home?"

'While I do not remember much between the hours of midnight and three o'clock, I do know during that stretch of time, I was in a comatose state and during most of it, was all alone. The very person I was laughing and having an enchanting time with decided to leave me in my sickly state to stomp off to the next bazaar; far from the drunken, pathetic woman who could not even hold her liquor."

"Did he really leave you alone? This surely is reminiscent of someone else. I hate to make such a harsh statement, but please tell me he was in a shattered, unfeeling, belligerent state of mind as well? Otherwise, I fear you are rehashing a past that you promised you would never accept as long as you live."

"Oh no, I most certainly am reliving a part of my life that always made me feel unbearably vulnerable. I am perfectly aware that I am solely responsible for my own actions, wise or intolerable, yet there is a part of me that yearns for that chivalrous man who desires to love me entirely for who I am and stand by me, for better or worse; in this case, worse being me embracing the 'ceramic goddess who engulfed my tumultuous affairs'. She most definitely would hold my secrets in the confines of her abyss."

"This paradox of two different worlds in which you are discussing is confusing. You live one life; that of an independent, self-reliant feminist who can do it all alone. Yet, you speak of an existence where the man you trust will not leave you behind in hopes of finding someone who is much more fun at the moment. Yesterday, you were complacent living within your own boundaries. Today, you dream of a gallant Odysseus who will lie beside you, both figuratively and literally, through all of life's joyous and dramatic happenings."

"Is all of this really too much to ask for?"

"Hmmm? I will have to ponder that one. The next day, did you wallow in self pity or did you pick yourself back up and start fresh, as the sun does."

"Wallow, of course. You should know me by now."

"What was the source of your wallowing, other than breaking someone's spirit and being left behind by your dream boat?"

"It never fails. Every time I go out and drink more than two margaritas or glasses of wine for that matter, I suffer the most disgusting consequences. Considering the fact that I drank a bottle of wine, god knows how many glasses of rum and coke, and I don't even remember how much ever clear, I was feeling a little under the weather the next day. My emotions and stomach were in a twisted knot. For the first time ever, I quietly sunk into my ever-forgiving couch and thawed my ice cold heart while becoming lost in four ridiculous, empty Hollywood hits that I was hoping would tear at my heart strings. No such luck."

"Your expectations are, as always, quite amusing. To believe Hollywood could undo the depravities of last night is absurd and entirely irrational. I would not expect anything less my dear, silly friend."

"There's that sarcasm again."

"My utmost apologies."

The Thirteenth Night

Feelings of inadequacy; too many to handle

"Life is a process of becoming, a combination of states we have to go through. Where people fail is that they wish to elect a state and remain in it. This is a kind of death."
~Anais Nin

"*T*onight, I just need you to hold me. No talking. No sighing. No disagreeing with my outlandish thoughts."

"You are desperate tonight. What happened to your newfound friend?"

'He is gone and I am again, both desperate and alone. I feel as if lately, or maybe my entire life, I have become impoverished by a lack of tender, supportive, genuine touch. While I have been falsely fulfilled by what, at this moment, seemed to be an artificial affection, I have lacked the kind of embrace that is safe and pure. I must be held."

"This may be difficult, as I am merely a voice and have no physical self in which to hold you with. Yet, whether or not you feel my embrace is entirely up to you."

"Please sit next to me so that I may feel your breath cut through this thick air and calm my heart."

"I have been sitting here all along. If you do not believe than I am here, and always have been, then you will never experience the kind of touch that may move you out of this realm of insanity that has plagued your life over the past year."

"If you are always here, then why do I so often feel completely alone?"

"Delving into the drudges of loneliness allows you to wholeheartedly enjoy each moment you are blessed by the solace of others. Being filled with the comfort and laughter of those around you comes from the remembrance that you have been entirely miserable and alone. This is one of the true paradoxes in life that we must come to terms with, no matter how much we want to disagree with it."

"I would love to sit here and discuss philosophy, psychology, and the meaning of life, but none of it is helping. I have been reading, studying, investigating, and plunging into countless self-help books in order to find a way out of this craze.

'Some insist that I must allow myself to feel this depravity, for it is the fourth step to healing.

'Others believe it is entirely beneficial to seek counsel from those around me whose lives have been affected by divorce.

'One even had the nerve to argue that it was all my fault; if I had prayed more, then my marriage would have worked. Like they had any clue how many nights I spent pleading with God that He would bring my husband home to be with his family. He did not come home, which I do not blame on Him, as free will was so kindly granted to us."

"There you go again, passing fault on the other half of the failure."

"I have come to a point in my life where I am finally able to admit my faults without feeling my heart tighten and my nerves go numb."

"Would you like to expand, since you are in such a depressed state of mind right now? You may as well carry on with it."

"Thank you so much for the concern and encouragement. You are most definitely improving my emotional state."

"That is my job."

"Why is it always so difficult to be humble? Sometimes I feel like a meteor hitting me in the head is more likely to happen than to have humility triumph over my pride, that miserable vice that seems to continually consume my consciousness. I finally understand why Mr. Lewis dedicated so many words to this subject, trying to get his readers to understand why it is so important to acknowledge self-importance and then tackle it head-on."

"I have had enough with your lack of humility. I know that it is a vice that you are so desperately trying to tackle, but please be real with me right now. What is really going on in your life? Does it have anything to do with your pancake-eating, tattooed bad boy with a compassionate heart that you at least envision encompasses his persona?"

"I hate that you are always so right on about everything; if all of us only had that luxury. We would all have it all together, wouldn't we?"

"A world of elitist know-it-alls. Sounds absolutely riveting."

"Actually, it sounds frightening. Your sarcasm, which I am forgiving at this moment due to the accompanying humor and playful tone, rings true for once.

'May we please continue our Travis discussion so that I may get some rest tonight?"

"So this is about the pancake guy."

"As a matter of fact, yes, it does have something to do with this man that everyone swears is not good for my soul. What do they know anyway? The one they believed was my soul mate turned out to be the very person whom I shared my heart with and then ran off with someone he believed, at that moment in time, was a better match for him."

"I have never seen you so angry before."

"Well, sadly for you, my incensed emotions do detonate with quite the outrageous force ever so often. You just happened to be the lucky onlooker who gets to experience such immature belligerence at this moment. I assure you it will be quite entertaining.

'I am in a nonsensical confusion, yet again. Being the raging, self-proclaimed feminist that I am, I swore I would never again allow myself to get so attached to someone. And still, yet again, I released all sense of control when it came to my innermost, raw emotions. I honestly believed that I could spend endless intimate hours with a man, meet his family, and then when we had enough, say goodbye with a smile on my face, embracing the beautiful memories we made under the stars.

'Dear lord, could I be any more ridiculous? As if I have the coldest, most hardened heart, which refuses to attach itself to any human being I share my deepest, darkest secrets with."

"I have learned much about you over these past months. I can undoubtedly say that you live your life as if you are subhuman. You may not be conscious of this fact, which could very well be argued, yet you seem to have this innate belief that you are beyond suffering; you are some superwoman who must have it all together at all times and who, in order to protect herself, can morph into this numb, unaffected being and leave her real self far behind."

'I know that I have alluded to the idea that I am a strong realist who understands life oh so clearly. As you may have discovered on this long, drawn out journey, I am a fickle, fragile, faded woman who, yet again, has succumbed to the very indulgent behaviors that I swore I would never give into; not even if Wentworth tried to tempt me with his piercing, enchanting eyes and endearing personality."

"You must be careful when describing everything that embodies you as a woman. Do not give into the self deprecation that too often plagues people's lives. While this may seem like a complete paradox, it may turn into the self indulgence that you have been trying so hard to fight against your entire young life.

'It is true that everyone, even those men and women who leave their legacy with us, carry with him or her an unequivocal sense of pride that may either plague humanity or better it. It is up to you to decide what you are going to do with it. If you succumb to the pressures of feelings sorry for yourself, delving into the trenches of self doubt and harsh criticism, then your pride will defeat you and you will never be that strong, loving woman that you must be."

"Must?"

"Do not forget that there is someone watching your every move, word, response to the world. If you act as if you have no raw feelings, she too will visit this floor as you have."

"What do I do with this pain? How do I overcome another loss? How do I protect her from all of this?"

"First, you must submit to the truth that it is perfectly okay to lose. You allowed yourself to be unexposed and trusted in someone who had a great impact on your life, even if you are still not with him. When you change your mind's perspective on loss, then your heart will follow suit."

"This does not make sense. How can my heart be content if I cannot be with someone I care for so dearly?"

"You will be continually touched by people's hearts if you allow yourself to be. This does not mean that they will stay with you and be an integral part of your daily conversations and on goings. You may never again hear their voice, embrace them, or be blessed by their company. And still, your heart will continually be filled with their presence because you have kept a space there for those who swiftly come in and out of your life, decorating it with different colors, designs, and eloquent ideas that may shake you to the point where the greatest revelation forces itself upon you. Do not desecrate your relationship with people just because you have closed off the very article of your life that houses the greatest of gifts just because you fear pain.

'You must also shake off this phony truth that you must always be strong. While you do an excellent job pretending to be the archetypal woman of strength and valor, I assure you this is not your destiny. I hate to be the one to disturb this fairytale that has subsisted in your mind for far too many years, yet being the discerning spirit that has been fated upon me, I promise when you give into the world of tears and pain, your life will be much easier. I also assure you that your little girl will be much less likely to put on this same mask that will indubitably harden her heart, leaving her susceptible to the throngs of pain that accompanies such a life of duplicity.

'The pressure, which may seem overbearing right now, will subside when you let go of your control and let your heart mourn. You will know when it is time to release this pain and instead find joy in your memories with someone who touched your life, even if for only a passing moment. He will not merely be a memory, as people come in to our lives and leave us just as quickly. What we do with that is completely up to us."

"You are telling me to relinquish control. Is this my third lesson of the night?"

"It most certainly is. That ex-husband of yours may not have been completely off base when he constantly asserted with such conviction that you are a control freak who cannot handle being immersed in every detail of her life."

"What has happened to my compassionate confidant?"

"Sometimes compassion and boldness must coexist in order to find truth. Also, a luminous author once wrote that when our hearts really want something, the entire universe will conspire to help your soul realize it. Your heart wants peace and if you allow others to help you, this may become your most freeing reality."

"My heart also wants to trust and to believe that it will love once again."

"You will love wholeheartedly. I cannot guarantee that it will be the romantic love that is spoken of in books and fairytales, but I do undoubtedly know that your heart will love. Besides, does it matter what type of love we give? I cannot help but shed tears of joy when I read Michelangelo's word's 'A life without love is no life at all'.

'You see, he does not isolate love or discuss between whom it must exist. I fear if he were to do that, the meaning of so strong a word, the exquisite requisite of life, would perish.

'Focus on those in your life who are so deserving of your love right now. That is where joy exists; not in trying to control your destiny or dwelling on loss. I fear if your focus lies on such trivial matters, as thousands have done, you too will never experience this true pleasure in life."

"Will you walk me through all of this? I fear there is so much to change that I will lose sight of what is most important and revert back to my old habits."

"I will be walking beside you, as I always do. Hopefully I will not be sitting here on this floor beside you for much longer."

"I am ready to find a more picturesque hangout too."

"Maybe soon?"

"I hope. Goodnight."

"Goodnight my love."

The Fourteenth Night

Do we really need one more Job?

*"Courage, it would seem, is nothing less than the power to overcome
danger, misfortune, fear, injustice, while continuing to affirm inwardly
that life with all its sorrows is good; that everything is meaningful even if
in a sense beyond our understanding; and that there is always tomorrow."*
~Dorothy Thompson

"**D**o you ever get sad?"

"What do you mean?"

"Have you ever felt so dejected that nothing, not even a child's laughter, could pull you out of the most dismal state of heart imaginable?"

"I am not quite sure where you are going with this. Are you finally succumbing to the most raw, innermost feelings that I have been so zealously trying to pull out of you all this time?"

"I am afraid that the strong, invincible woman who sits before you has become what she has always feared most.

'Shakespeare so keenly discussed the seven ages of man; first an infant, then a child, a teenager, an adult, a forty-something, a wise old man or woman, and then again a vulnerable, weak child, surrendering to nature's most bizarre ways.

'I feel as if I have surpassed all of the middle stages and have prematurely yielded to her harsh, yet natural manner. I have become, once again, a helpless newborn who cannot even fathom getting off of this floor and facing the harsh, cruel world that I once believed consisted only of innately good people who desired to love unconditionally, under any circumstance and without question.

'I have obviously been sorely mistaken. As my students would say, the ids are taking over the world. No more superegos-Mother Theresas, Ghandis, Abrahams; just hordes of walking ids whose pure consciences, let alone hearts, have not been given the golden opportunity to become fully developed."

"Maybe your perceptions are just tainted. Don't you remember what your favorite poet once argued about this truth? One of her greatest convictions was the reality that perceptions cause the downfall of a person's character. With this said, maybe your assessment of those of around you is jaded because of the recent experiences you have unwontedly encountered over this past year."

"Like she had a clue? Pretty soon, I am going to be just like her-secluded and alone; locked up in a space that consists of me and my books."

"It is strange how quickly you change your opinions on such passionate matters that used to satiate your heart. That woman, who you have all of a sudden chosen to negate as a person and a writer, was able to dig out the very particles that molded her soul and truly *feel* them. Has that not always been your dream—to experience what it is like to turn inside out and see the reflection that stands before you?

'You cannot allow that cynical part of your heart to terrorize your thoughts and win over the most critical aspect of your life."

"And may I ask what that is?"

"Your ability to see through the dingiest, darkest situations and see what is good—truly good."

"Do you truly believe that *good* even exists?"

"Do you? Look at *her*. Is she not beautiful, loving, compassionate? Does she not look at a rainbow and become awestruck at the fact that some great Artist was able to take His paintbrush and color in the lines so perfectly?"

"I cannot look at her and see anything but good. Still I fear that ten, twenty, thirty years from now, the days and then years will steal all that innocence from her little soul and make her hard. This decay of pure laughter and naivety seems to instill in us the inability to look at those colorful streaks across the sky the same way. What once was an intoxicating miracle becomes a flash of color that becomes erased from our hearts in one fleeting moment of reality."

"It doesn't have to be that way."

"Please, my romantic friend, explain to me the easy way out of this absurdity."

"While it is most certainly not simple, it is attainable.

'First, you must get off of that floor. Your really are starting to look quite pathetic.

'Go take a quick look in the mirror. I know, your saggy...eyes, rash-stricken face, and rooted hair might momentarily take away any thoughts of 'goodness', yet you will get past that."

"Promise?"

"Trust me; your sad appearance is the least of your worries right now. We must get to the bottom of the upside down world that you have created in your mind.

'Then, Ms. Feeblecorn, look at the young woman—you are still young, even in Shakespearean years—and think of what you saw when you were twenty-two."

"I had horrible acne, no idea what I was going to do with my life, and a failed engagement."

"I know all that. I want you to think of how you pictured the world. Think of that wretched three-hour-long train ride in the smoking car in Italy with Rebekah. Think of being stuck between the two train cars with that sweaty Italian couple making out in 100-degree temperatures and the endless drops of sweat pouring down your face as you stood in disgust for two, long hours. Recall the night you were lost in Venice and every turn led you to the sewer-filled water; no bridges in sight.

'If I would have asked you in the midst of any of those moments what your view of humanity was, you would have answered in the politest way possible, 'Human beings are innately good and life is just as it should be."

"Don't you thing those situations are a bit different from the one that haunts me now?"

"Aren't you the one who has always believed that pain and loss are all relative?"

"Yes. Where are going with this?"

"While many believe those memories of physical torment cannot be even slightly compared to a divorce, they can give you insight into the person who fought through them with laughter, a sense of humor, and an appreciative heart that she was alive to even experience such moments. Only five years ago, you were a resilient woman who loved anything life brought her. You could not have left that woman behind on foreign soil."

"I came home with the same heart that summer."

"You have the same heart still. It has just aged slightly, but it still sees flecks of light trying to form a brilliant radiance that will emerge from such a dark, sad passage in life."

"What is the third thing I must do?"

"I just told you."

"No, you passed up that one."

"Your heart."

"My heart? What do I do with it?"

"Let it breathe, as you once did. You hold on to it so tight that it cannot even let the smallest, most beautiful idea survive within your most precious asset—my most precious asset.

'And constantly remind yourself of what you truly believed when you were *her* age and when you were even twenty-two; that goodness, graciousness, kindness is inevitable.

"One last thing, you must rid yourself of too much realism. It will kill your spirit."

"Utopia it is."

"That is more like it."

"Goodnight."

"Dream of your Utopia."

"Well, I am going to need your help. I seem to have been living in my own dystopia for some time now and believing there is a world out there where peace actually permeates hearts is a completely irrational thought."

"Of course it is."

The Fifteenth Night
All alone

"I have learned two lessons in my life: first, there are no sufficient literary, psychological, or historical answers to human tragedy, only moral ones. Second, just as despair can come to one another only from other human beings, hope, too, can be given to one only by other human beings."
~Elie Wiesel

"**P**lease tell me I am not going to be completely alone the rest of my life."

"Well, first you must define *alone*."

"I do not want to think tonight. It is always, passion or reason, good or evil, just or unjust, the external or the internal. Tonight, I just want to be given the answer. I do not want to spend hours brooding over an either or an or.

"This is who you are. You would not find any happiness in skimming the surface, barely touching the very paradoxes and ironies that nourish your soul."

"Yes, but the problem lies in the inconsistencies that seem to plague my life.

'You see, there are days when I am perfectly content realizing that my reality might be much like Jane's. While I will never compare to her humility or her grace for that matter, my fate may be much like hers. Many will say that Ms. Austin, who 'lived by the pen', breathed an accomplished, selfless, incandescent life.

'Yet, even Jane, who epitomized the passionate, uncompromising, independent woman of her time, aspired for that which we all dream of, love. I am not speaking of the kind of love that satisfies our loneliness for the time being, as I have experienced on more than one occasion. I dream of the kind of love that one cannot even pen and give justice to."

"Have you experienced such?"

"I am blessed to say that I did love once. While it was unrequited, it was love nonetheless."

"Unrequited? Like loneliness, you might want to first know what love is. The definition of love may be unique to each heart, as our experiences tend to form our theories on such esteemed matters."

"I would be fighting my deepest convictions if I did not say that love, which is the most remarkable of achievements, should always be given the highest honors. Even the great Artist esteems this as the all-encompassing means to meeting Him face to face upon the end of our journey.

'Our purpose, as imperfect human beings, is to love. It is to make ourselves susceptible to ultimate loss. Love makes each and every one of us entirely defenseless, invincible, exposed.

'While I should be rejoicing in the fact that I have experienced such vulnerability and devotion, I find myself lying here, not able to move."

"Have you become deadened to any such ideology that, formerly, you so passionately held to be truth?"

"Yes."

"Is this your emotional, fickle self emerging, again? Or, have you taken on a new philosophy about this *thing* that you used to discuss so passionately?"

"I wish my principles, which lately seem to adjust according to my sentiments of the day, were written in stone. Some days, upon reading awe-inspiring treatise on this topic, I am irrevocably drawn to the idea that soon, I will look into the eyes of a man and know that this potent, commanding force will draw the two of use together.

'Then, I find myself disgusted with such a romantic idea. Even Shakespeare, who may not have been the best expert on love, leaving his second best bed to his wife (what a scandal), wrote of this very edifice that desires the unaltered attention of the human condition. It seems as if nearly every character consecrated to such perfection must undergo the worst of plagues in order to find or carryout their love. This cannot be true.

'Then I wonder was Jane in fact contented because she did experience love; even if she was not able to see his face, except in short, ephemeral encounters where their love was to remain anonymous? This just does not seem fair."

"You seem discontented that your romantic idea of love is not shared by all. Do you really believe that everyone must find their perfect soul mate, as you modernists call it, and live happily ever after?"

"Of course, that is what is fed to us from early childhood."

"By Hollywood. Do you really want to take advice on so important a subject from a dreamland that cannot even hold two of their stars together for more than a few months?"

"Point well taken."

"Love must not be handled with such carelessness. While you may be broken right now, and your view on this matter may have become quite infected, there is a pure, unadulterated beauty that encompasses this distinguished necessity in life."

"While I can admire your unsullied, genuine dissertation on love, I must say that I have, in fact, become tainted. To be honest, I am not sure I will ever be able to put myself at risk and give my heart to a man again. I would love to be impervious and hand over my emotions, knowing that they may become dejected when least expected."

"As I said before, that heart is not yours. You have been completely blinded in this area. I am tempted to say that maybe this is the source of your so-called failure."

"I am really not sure how to respond to such a bold statement. I think you may have just overstepped your boundaries."

"Boldness, yes. Boundaries, no. I am your friend and you must hear this, as there are many people who may want to bring this to your attention, yet out of fear they remain silent only to protect their own pride.

'You are hiding behind the theory that you have control over your heart. While you are partially correct in one area, you are dreadfully mistaken in an even more crucial one; one that, if recognized, will lead you to utmost joy.

'Now I do not want to make it sound like there is a Utopian world out there than can be grasped in an instant once you have comprehended the truths that I am ready to lay out before you."

"We all know More's purpose in writing his great book was not to trick us into believing such a world exists on earth, where men are running around murdering, cheating, lying, and participating in all other vile activities that only man is capable of."

"Yes, but do you know that this cynicism that used to only abide among the adults, has captured and held hostage the very person who you once swore would not exist. You, my dear companion, have succumbed to the pressures of an adult world that breeds suspicion, realism, distrust. What happened to the boa constrictor inside the hat? Apparently, that does not exist for you anymore either. When you adhere to these two following truths, then you may return to a world in which the Little Prince was not just a figment of your imagination."

"Please, do tell my oh-so-brilliant accomplice to this harsh crime against love that I apparently have committed."

"First, you must define what is good in order to find love. Goodness is only achieved through our great Artist, who has defined this ideology for us in black and white in His great novel. We alone are not capable of good at all, as Kierkegaard argued.

'Once we have defined what is good, we must then define faith. My great friend, we must not trust man, as he is entirely prone to failure."

"Are you telling me I have putting all of my time and energy into something that will never be secure no matter how delicately I nourish it?"

"While love endures, it also falls short, as human beings err. If you exert all of your emotions and time into man, then you will become broken. Your faith, which a wise man once defined as a 'Reasoned response to the initiation of the great Artist,' must be untouched in order to find any joy in your life. Without the knowledge of what is good and in what to have faith, love will never fully exist for you."

"Then why are we given such human, womanly emotions that tear at us until our hearts ache so much that we withdraw completely from everything around us that is good?"

"I would love to give you a cliché response, such as, 'It is because you are human.' Yet, that clashes with all of my convictions. It is because you have not surrendered completely to the ultimate sacrifice of your Artist and made His abounding love your reality. You have looked for goodness, faith, and love in man. I assure you, this is not where you will find it. You will fail, miserably."

"What about those women out there who have attained joy in men?"

"Their joy is a farce; a sham to protect their fictitious sense of pride. Your Artist, your rescuer who you discuss on numerous occasions, told us once that those who trust in man are foolish."

"So what do I do, not trust in men at all?"

"I have laid it out before you. Your expectations and perceptions will ruin those around you. Do not you remember one of your favorite

Dickenson poems about the damnation that Perceptions, which become personified, do to people? They will guide you to a life of loneliness and bitterness.

'While there are certain acts that man executes against man that are not justifiable and oftentimes lead to ominous ends, there are times in our lives where forgiveness overpowers the depraved act that led to heartache."

"Are you saying I should not have divorced a man who fell under the deceitful category?"

"Not at all. I am saying that from now on, I advise you to put your faith elsewhere. I am not promising that you will fall into agape love with the man of your dreams down the road, yet you will experience the type of love that can only be shared by a Creator and His child. This is where the real basis of life exists, in the arms of an invincible, adoring, loving friend who will never betray you.

"And, if a man comes along someday whose Perceptions do not ruin you, and him for that matter, than you are doubly blessed. If they do not, rest assure in the fact that the most ardent, beautiful love waits for you."

"I will rest peacefully tonight on the reassurance of this reality that I have stifled my entire adult life."

"You should draw your boa constrictor from inside and out tonight. It will no longer be a hat for you, my friend. Please promise me you will teach her your illustration as well. Do not let her forget it."

"This will be my ambition."

"Good night, my love."

"Good night."

The Last Night
Shutting the door

"Then, without realizing it, you try to improve yourself at the start of each new day; of course, you achieve quite a lot in the course of time. Anyone can do this, it costs nothing and is certainly very helpful. Whoever doesn't know it must learn and find by experience that a quiet conscience makes one strong."
~Anne Frank

"*O*k, I know it has been a few weeks since I last beckoned you to this jaded life of mine. But as the wise Little Prince one suggested, if you tame someone, they will be your faithful friend for eternity. You have succeeded, immensely. Therefore, I will call you my ever-loyal companion and will ask that you grace me with your omniscient presence just one more time.

'I know in our last meeting I said I did not need you anymore. I, in all of my proud glory, thought I could not only face my demons alone, but rather bump them off one lowly imp at a time. I clearly was wrong.

'Remember that Rose the devoted Prince loved so unconditionally? Well I have become her; self-conceited, whiny, and alone. I will admit coming to terms with this reality shook me to the very core. Upon realizing that I was everything that I could not stand, I was awakened to the truth that being sad, disheartened to the point of sheer insanity, cannot be tackled alone. Therefore, I am asking for your comfort, yet again, to help ameliorate this raw, excruciating pain that burns through my entire body."

"I told you, I am always here, waiting for you to ask me to be your companion when you have fallen into the murky, bleak pit of sorrow. My goodness, hanging out with you has likened me to one of those sappy novels you despise so much. I must change my tone of voice. And, if I do not begin choosing my adjectives much more carefully as well, I am going to be down there on that pathetic floor with you."

"You and your sarcasm. It has really started to grow on me."

"I knew it would. I know you say you are sad and in distress, but your eyes seem different this morning. I won't go so far as to liken them to Athena's, but they seem to have more of a glint to them than usual."

"You know, my eyes used to be the one feature of mine that people noticed more than any of the others. Apparently, they possessed a certain sheen to them that made people believe they could truly see my soul. I suppose, at that time in my life (the one where I was much more sound), I was pretty transparent and my eyes did glisten, quite frequently. However, over the past twelve months, I have only had one person even allude to the fact that my eyes highlighted my true character.

'Needless to say, after that ridiculous rant, I am indebted to you for bringing back to life what I once lost."

"I truly embrace every crazy moment spent with you. I would be appreciative if you would tell me the reason for our reunion on this blistery, snow-drenched morning and explain to me why this is the last conversation we will have…until next time."

"I am praying there will not be a next time, and if there is, of course I will leap at the opportunity to be graced by your refreshing presence.

'You see, while I say this morning will be our last conversation, it is not the end of a rapturous friendship. I realized today (sorry it took so long) that you have been with me since the inception of my one-year sabbatical from sanity. As a matter of fact, you have been with me since the great inauguration of my life. Why it took me twenty-seven years to realize it? You most likely have a much better answer to that question than I do. Nonetheless, the origin of my almost-Athena-like eyes stem from this illustrious awareness."

"I must ask, what helped guide you to this truth?"

"Tears! Many of them."

"While you have sulked, whined, and moped below the poppies for months now, I have not seen you cry but more than twice. I always knew you were not some calloused, bitter woman who would be numb the rest of her life."

"You seem absolutely jovial at the very thought of seeing me shed tears."

"Since I am now your sincere, loving friend, I must be honest. I am thrilled to see you cry."

"My dear friend, you are not the first to admit to such a harsh reality. Although you could have been more scrupulous in the way you worded your feelings, I am grateful that you are always so candid and real with me.

'The source of my tears may sound completely ridiculous to you, especially when you realize the very foundation from which they stem.

Yet, since you love me, even after knowing all of my imperfections, I will not leave out one detail.

'I actually woke up feeling quite affable yesterday morning. I got out of bed, turned on the ever-reliable coffee pot, opened the curtains, and to my surprise there was a white covering of snow extending throughout the picturesque landscape in front of me. I could sense that this blanket of the utmost pure, untainted gift of nature was going to be symbolic of the new journey on which I was going to embark. After all, one year ago today I finally made the decision to suspend a marriage that had no grounds for remaining in tact.

'Some may argue that it was unscathed and that I had no right to timidly ascend to the peak of those daunting stairs that creep into the very edifice of doom and hand over the termination of a decree that I promised I would never break. My god, obtaining that stamp made me feel like I was supposed to go out and sew myself a scarlet letter and fasten it to my breast for the rest of eternity.

'Nonetheless, my fate (if I believe in such a thing, I am not yet certain), was sealed. While hearing that dreaded sound of black ink, which seems so miniscule in other aspects of our mundane lives, collide with the paper that held my entire life's future in its hands, I was besieged; held captive by the most painful sensation that has ever ravaged my heart. To my surprise, only hours later my distressing torment turned into something I have never before felt; frozen.

'You see, this numbness that has taken over this past year has been completely unfeigned. I have been told by some that it is not normal or reasonable to feel numb. For emotions must always accompany different stages of our lives. Joy complements times where life seems to fall perfectly into place; the birth of a child, a wedding day, finally getting the job of our dreams, our in-laws moving far, far away from existence. Sadness accompanies the times in our lives where the universe seems to be in a complete craze; the loss of a loved one, a job, a home, a self.

'I have found over the past year, that this whole idea of being completely anesthetized, deadened to any kind of emotion that accompanies the kind of pain where our world is frozen to the point of not truly knowing in which direction to move, is exceedingly real. I have become aware of the authentic truth that lies between coming to terms with this bizarre irony and awakening to who we really are and what lies before us.

'If I had not been able to accept the fact that this paradoxical notion of having a numb sensation was going to grow me into a stronger, more sane woman some day, then I would not be here sharing my reality with you, dear friend. I also may not be able to sit here, on this gloomy floor and embrace a year of complete madness."

"The first night I met you, there were no tears. There were definite hurts, aches, and a bitter dejection that suffocated the room. I knew from the onset that you were going to hit a plethora of emotions, yet the one that would flood your spirit would be the one that is deadened and dull.

'There were so many times when I wanted to awaken you to this truth. Yet I knew you would find it completely idealistic and would therefore have built a wall between me, your rational friend, and you, the naïve, out-of-reach woman who built herself a barrier between the world and herself. I am contented to see that you have shoveled, or rather, fought your way from the dark realm that you had created and have decided to turn yourself inside out and hold firm to that which is unequivocally real; your unaffected, valid conviction that you truly know what holds credence when faced against a world that tries to instill in us principles that are not our own."

"You may laugh at what guided me to this raw truth that if we are not utterly confident in what we stand for, then we become mystified when faced with the daunting question of who we *really* are. Now, it is no question that this epiphany took longer to surface for me than for many others who have become entangled in the unforgiving world of divorce. While I could look back on this past year with regret and dissatisfaction that I did not handle it with grace and beauty, I am delighted that I have emerged out of my solitude to unearth, not regain, an assurance that I will stand with a poise that has never before escorted my personae.

'Again, this may sound completely juvenile, but if it is what led me to this awareness, then it must surface. Looking back on this past year, I know this new insight into my true character has been forming since the onset of my physical and spiritual separation from a person

I promised to love and cherish for eternity. I had much more strength than I ever credited myself.

'Yet, it was through four short incoming text messages and one tranquil reply that I realized conquering the ever-violent foe, insanity, would take many more raised brows and less and less cowering shoulders.

'My cherished friend Travis, whom I have discussed on occasion, let me in on a secret about myself that I had suppressed for years.

'While sitting in the Bay Area, contemplating his life's journey and whether or not he was content with it, he decided to let me in on a newfound reality of his. In his short thesis, he revealed that he had started seeing someone new and that because of our attraction for one another and my exclusiveness while we were dating, that he had to be honest out of respect for me. He was kind, gentle, and compassionate, adjectives that do not normally accompany such a revelation. While his intentions may have been to get rid of this crazy conservative before Election Day, instead of helping me gain a new perspective on the world, he unknowingly served as a bridge that would help me pass between the underworld of insanity and the ephemeral, quizzical, yet enchanting life that I truly believe was intended for all of us.

'In my short, yet serene conversation with this man I had only known for a few months, the words flowed. Our language was eloquent and candid, both admitting that our complete differences were enough to put a halt to any relationship. He was truthful about where he stood in life and thankful that I was not like the other crazy girls he dated who went into a state of psychosis at the very thought of him with another woman (if he had only known that all of my psychotic energy had been expended elsewhere).

'He did not falter in his convictions and was unapologetic for who he was and what he stood for. This is the very quality that first drew me to him. I, on the other hand, did not handle myself with as much grace as our conversation started to draw to a close. Thankfully, he did not let this fault of mine go unnoticed. He could have ignored it, feeling sorry for me as I stumbled to find the words to say. I told him that it would be completely unfair to want someone to be alone and that I was very happy for him. For he was a great catch (Yes, I used the horrific cliché that would make me run far away from someone if they dare use it against me). Then, after discussing how dissimilar we were, I likened myself to a prude."

"Those are harsh words, even for someone who does not cry much and who, before this Travis came in the picture, had only shared herself with one other man."

"Ok, funny guy, I am trying to get to the gist of this valuable story."

"Moving along…"

"Upon likening myself to someone who stuffs their nose up to the heavens, giving off the air of condescension and haughtiness, he quickly corrected me."

"Apparently, you need to do a quick refresher course on the correct usage of the every-day adjectives."

"Thank you, smart guy. Remember, I am the English teacher, which, yet again, automatically makes me radiate brilliance."

"You are being sarcastic now, my sarcasm-is-my-worst-enemy-friend."

"As I was saying, Travis told me that it was admirable that I knew what I stood for. No matter what reality was at hand, I was unwavering in my convictions. This is something to be cherished, not frowned upon, as I have done on numerous occasions.

'Upon this realization of the negative connotation this word held, I finally recognized that under no circumstances should I apologize for who I am and what I stand for, even if it is not held in popular belief that it is true or attainable.

'While many tears were shed after saying goodbye through our awkward means of communication (which I never was able to explain), I was elated that this could-have-been unnerving discourse on how to end a quasi-relationship was so peaceful. I was even happier to realize, after a few hours, that this dialogue between two completely different people helped me see that the only way to find the balance between infinite bliss and utter despondency is to really turn ourselves inside out and become fully raw, not masking any principles or passions we hold in the core of our souls. There must not be any apologizing accompanied with the revelation of these agencies of truth either."

"I am not surprised after all of your trepidations you have crawled through this past year, that four measly text messages enlightened you to the point of self-realization and then, sanity."

"My dear friend, you stand corrected. You see, saying goodbye to him was a lesson in itself and taught me much about my resilience, rationality, and delicate heart. While I owe much to him for helping me see the world through a different pair of eyes, I still cannot give away that which is undoubtedly mine."

"And might I ask what *is* yours."

"My tears, my joy, my experiences, my insanity, my rationality, and most important-my heart.

'It was with me all along. I just had to endure belligerent storms to finally make it here. I will miss you dearly. Yet, I know I will always find comfort in the promise that my life will be forever wrapped in your perfect, unadulterated love."

"Until next time my dear friend."

"Until next time."

Afterward

"Man must evolve for all human conflict a method which rejects revenge, aggression and retaliation. The foundation of such a method is love."
~Martin Luther King, Jr.

*J*t is appalling to look back on twelve years and realize that much of my existence was fraught with a quasi-reality that unknowingly satiated my life. Yet, what is even more scandalous is the sudden epiphany that in my heart I really knew what my reality was all along. Having to admit this truth took countless hours, which consisted of unraveling a myriad of layers that ultimately concealed the authentic, vulnerable woman who lie beneath the resilient, impenetrable, independent surface.

While peeling off these disguises was daunting and forced me to a place "where there is no darkness", I have broken out of my day-after-day fight with insanity. This is not to say that I do not still sit underneath my grandmother's painting, crying incessantly for some sense of normality. It also certainly does not mean I have it "all together" and am in the most perfect, pristine place in life. And I most assuredly am not implying that I walk with my head held high and embrace each moment with a whole heart in tact at all times.

No one emerges out of a divorce, or any heart-wrenching impasse in his or her life, completely whole. We become broken, downtrodden, exposed.

For months, I was handed so many books on how to get through a divorce. Happy endings seemed to be the theme that permeated the endless pages of these fairytale textbooks. While some of them had some really great advice, I was still at a loss as to how to graduate from one step to the next. My sense of failure (which I can only blame on myself) heightened and I found myself delving deeper into my insane state of mind.

It was then that I realized I had to get through this in a different way than what I had been taught. I definitely had to find an unconventional method of facing this demoralizing situation that was looming over me for such a long time. After the first night of sitting on my floor, I found a sense of peace and healing that I had been waiting for so long. I am not sure if it was the talking to myself piece, the comfort of being underneath my grandmother's beautiful work of art (which she created in the midst of insanity), or just the divulging of my greatest fears to my great Artist, that I was able to start emerging out of the pain and solitude that walked with me during this agonizing part of my life. The realization that I was not "sane" helped keep the numbness from crawling through my layers and piercing the one part of my body that holds my purpose and my unadulterated self. It was crucial that I protect my heart. The strange paradox is I was not the one truly shielding it from becoming empty-the voice on the other end of my mind, heart, soul was there to redirect the steps my mind tried so ardently to take.

I am not saying that I am completely proud of the decisions I made while on my "road to sanity". There were times where I was rash, impulsive, and just plain juvenile. Letting it all go is not always the best solution to dealing with pain and rejection. I made some very poor choices, had to deal with the consequences, and will most likely always feel the effects of my insanity. Still, I have the serenity in my promised redemption.

The acceptance of all of this-brokenness, responsibility, and healing-is what will help me find joy and a sense of self in my life. Purging it all and then pretending it never existed, or does not still exist, will lead me right back to where I sat for so many hours, days, weeks, in my small, isolated room.

Yes, I will always still ask questions: Why does pain exist? Does free will triumph over fate? How can bad actually win over good? Why did this happen? Am I always going to be alone?

The difference between then and now is that I do not have to know the answers. There's no reason for me to be angry with the person on the other side of my pain. I can finally be contented with the fact that I am here, a single, 28-year-old divorcee, without the gallant man of her dreams who swept her off her feet on his glorious stallion and rode her into her pristine, sunset setting. I am real life at its best...why would I not embrace this truth and live each moment with all of my heart-broken or not? It would be an absolute tragedy at its best to waste my heart on numbness, anger, or yesterday for that matter. People come into our lives to teach us, to guide us, to give us some kind of reflection of ourselves. If nothing more, this is what *he* gave me, and for that I am thankful. It is my turn to take that sane part of my personae and live wholeheartedly-no more polluting the air around me with distorted thoughts that will darken my light.

This journey has given me hope that no matter what pain enters our lives, it will become dissolved and only the small, leftover particles will occasionally emerge and guide us off course. When they do, we will know how to grasp them, listen to them, and regain our greatest sense of direction; one we had no clue existed before raw pain shattered our hearts and plunged us into insanity.

This past year, as I have also learned, was no fault of anyone's but my own. While my husband did make certain choices, it was completely up to me how I was going to let that impact my life. Was I going to hold a grudge, internalize the pain, move on as if nothing happened? Or, was I going to accept my responsibility in this failure and admit to the fact that I will always have a part of me that is broken and that will never completely mend? I will always carry my divorce with me and all of the other difficult sagas in my life. I will always fight between a world of awareness and numbness. This is my reality.

Acknowledgments

My land of women

My life has been shaped, inspired, and blessed by the beautiful, compassionate women who have always so ardently stood beside me. While this past year was filled with much heartache and loss, it was also satiated with laughter and an over-abundance of joy and hope. This all transpired from the most passionate, lovely group of women.

Mom~My most exquisite, passionate, resilient mother. I have watched life crumble before you and have been in awe at how graceful, humble, and optimistic you are. I have always found the greatest reassurance in your love and my life has been exceedingly blessed by your constant shoulder on which I have so often cried. I am not sure I could have broken through the chalice steels of insanity without your voice, your heart, your patience. Now that I am somewhat rational, I can say that while we are alone in a traditional sense of the world, we have more than any woman can ask for-our crazy, sensitive, most loving family. We are eternally blessed.

Aunt Annie~Your eccentric persona and fake flowers will always be etched into my soul. There is no other woman on earth as feisty and at the same time, as compassionate and giving as you. You are the rock of our family and have instilled in me the yearning to move forward and be as strong as I know I can be. I love you infinitely.

Hailey~My most beautiful, creative, energetic friend. I always prayed for a little sister and I never would have guessed that I would get a mini-me as lovely and as full of life as you. You have endured life with me over these past few years and I am so thankful you were there. God's timing could not have been more perfect.

Michaela~Your grace, gentle spirit, and benevolence will forever be imprinted in my soul. I have never known a person who listens with her whole heart and loves everyone so unconditionally. Every day I am eternally grateful for your friendship. You epitomize what it means to be a true friend, a woman of strength, and a mother. I know that so many lives will be touched by your fervent love, selflessness, and tender heart.

Courtney~I will never forget the first time I actually cried to you. I still laugh when I think of how elated you were to see tears flowing down my puffy, soiled cheeks. Some may find this completely sardonic, yet I find the reassurance of a most beautiful, devoted, paramount friendship. When my heart was in complete shambles, you never failed to comfort me, even from so far away. I love you with all of heart my bestest. I pray that one truth you will always accept is that you will make marriage beautiful, selfless, and eternal.

Rebekah~My lovely Rebekah. Some of my most treasured moments are centered around the most beautiful settings: The colorful streets of Venice, the moonlight on the Italian Riviera, the picturesque hillsides of Switzerland, the cobblestone streets of Dijon. While each setting is proof of God's graciousness and profound artistic capability, nothing proves His munificence more than the very person I was able to experience such beauty with. My heart, which was shaped so much with you by my side, will always be yours.

The men who give me hope

Of course there were times over this past year when my faith in the male race came to a startling halt. Yet, I must admit that while I wanted to denounce men altogether, there were a number of men in my life who gave me faith in my time of dejection and complete solitude.

Anthony~My rebellious, sensitive, free-spirited little brother. I have watched you evolve into the most kind-hearted, hard-working, passionate man over this past year. I know life has never been easy for you and at times, the world seemed to be waging war against your hopes and dreams. I am amazed at how you fought it all head-on and have risen above the labels, the pain, and the solitude. You are superman.

Josh~Your ever-present love and faith in me has been a source of my strength over the past year. I love you with my whole heart and I know that underneath that tough persona, there lies a man who will break down the very barriers that have divided us from those we love. I have always known that my littlest brother would fight extremely tough storms. I didn't realize that through those times of turbulence, you would evolve into who you have become. You have given me faith. I love you.

Steve~My most favorite uncle in the whole world. What would this family be like without you? Your virtue, strength, and unadulterated love have always helped guide us through the most difficult and most beautiful times in our lives. You are our man of strength.

My muse~My dear friend. Your confidence in me and my story has been my source of inspiration over the past year. I have shared my joys, my hopes, my laughter, and my tears with you and have been eternally blessed by the way you see the world. You always seem to find what is most beautiful, in both nature and humanity. I have learned so much from you and I hope I have returned that gift to you as well. Love, Edna with a life vest.

My students
While there are days where our class can be likened to complete mayhem, it has ironically been a source of serenity for me. How could I not be inspired by your empathy, joyous spirits, and eagerness to be stirred by what I have to teach you and even better, by what you have to teach each other? I am exactly where I am supposed to be.

www.ingramcontent.com/pod-product-compliance
Lightning Source LLC
Chambersburg PA
CBHW020248290526
45784CB00003B/1154